JOURNEYINK

Brugge Travel Guide 2025

Discover Hidden Gems, Budget Tips, and Local Secrets for an Unforgettable Trip

Copyright © 2025 by JourneyInk

All rights reserved. No part of this publication may be reproduced, stored or transmitted in any form or by any means, electronic, mechanical, photocopying, recording, scanning, or otherwise without written permission from the publisher. It is illegal to copy this book, post it to a website, or distribute it by any other means without permission.

First edition

This book was professionally typeset on Reedsy.
Find out more at reedsy.com

Contents

Welcome to Brugge	1
Introduction to the City	1
A Brief History of Brugge	2
Why Visit Brugge in 2025?	3
What's New in Brugge for 2025?	4
Essential Travel Tips	7
Best Time to Visit Brugge	7
Currency and Local Customs	9
Where to Exchange Currency	12
Language and Communication Tips	13
The Language Situation in Brugge	13
Practical Tips for Communication	14
Useful Phrases in Dutch/Flemish	14
Using Basic English	17
Language Etiquette	17
Cultural Considerations	18
Safety Tips and Essential Resources	19
Safety Tips and Local Etiquette	19
Health and Emergency Information	21
Useful Apps and Resources	23
Getting to Brugge	26
Arriving by Plane	26
Arriving by Train	29
Navigating Brugge	32
How to Get Around the City	32
Taxi Services and Day Trips	38

Taxi Services and Ride-Sharing Apps	38
Day Trips	41
Where to Stay in Brugge	44
Luxury Hotels	44
Boutique & Great-Value Stays	46
Budget-Friendly Hotels and Unique Places to Stay	50
Affordable Comfort and Convenience	50
Hostels, Guesthouses, and More	52
Dining in Brugge	56
Must-Try Local Delights	56
Top Restaurants for Every Budget	60
Belgian Beer and Cafes	63
Exotic Belgian beers	63
Cafes & Bistros	66
Vegan Options and Local Markets	69
Vegetarian and Vegan Options in Brugge	69
Street Food and Local Markets	73
Must-See Sights in Brugge	76
Historic Sites and Landmarks	76
Exploring Brugge's Canals	80
Museums and Galleries	82
Exploring Brugge's Canals	86
Off-the-Beaten-Path	88
Hidden Gems to Explore	88
Local Shops and Unique Finds	91
Brugge for Families	94
Kid-Friendly Attractions	94
Romantic Activities for Couples	100
Love-Filled Activities	100
Entertainment and Nightlife	106
Best Bars and Pubs	106
Live Music Venues and Events	109
Cinemas, Nightclubs, and Dance Spots	112

Theatrical Shows and Cinemas	112
Nightclubs and Dance Spots	114
Local Festivals and Events	118
Shopping in Brugge	124
Local Souvenirs	124
Best Shops for Antiques and Collectibles	127
Designer Stores and Street Fairs	130
Boutiques, Fashion, and Designer Stores	130
Brugge's Markets and Street Fairs	133
Where to Find Unique Artisan Goods	135
Outdoor Activities and Recreation	138
Cycling Tours and Rentals in Brugge	138
Walking Tours	141
Parks and Scenic Views in Brugge	144
Parks and Green Spaces in Brugge	144
Scenic Views and Photography Spots	147
Water Sports	151
Water Sports and Canal Activities	151
Day Trips from Brugge	156
Ghent	156
The Coastline	159
Brussels and The Flemish Countryside	163
A Day in the Capital	163
Peaceful Getaways	166
Itineraries for Every Type of Traveler	170
One Day in Brugge	170
A Romantic Weekend	174
Brugge with Kids and Cultural Exploration	177
A Family-Friendly Adventure	177
A Cultural Exploration of Brugge's Art and History	179
Food Lover's Weekend and Scenic Escape	183
A Food Lover's Weekend	183
A Relaxing, Scenic Brugge Escape	186

Practical Information for Travelers	189
Currency and Money	189
Local Emergency Numbers and Services	191
Travel Insurance and Staying Connected	195
Travel Insurance Tips	195
SIM Cards and Wi-Fi	198
Accessibility for Disabled Travelers and FAQ	201
Accessibility for Disabled Travelers	201
Answers to Common Travel Questions	205
Appendices	208
List of Local Festivals and Events in 2025	208
Directory of Key Attractions and Services	210
Travel Resources and Further Reading	213

Welcome to Brugge

Brugge, known as the "Venice of the North," is a small yet captivating city in Belgium. It's famous for its cobblestone streets, winding canals, and medieval architecture. Set in the northwest of Belgium, Brugge is a city that feels like it's been frozen in time, yet it continues to evolve and thrive, making it a perfect destination for tourists in 2025.

Introduction to the City

In 2025, Brugge remains one of the most visited cities in Europe, drawing travelers for its picturesque streets, historic landmarks, and unique charm. Unlike many other cities that have modernized extensively, Brugge has managed to maintain its medieval character, with much of its city center still looking much like it did hundreds of years ago. Visitors will find themselves walking along canals that have been there for centuries, crossing over bridges that offer postcard-perfect views of the city's towering bell tower, the Belfry of Brugge, and its colorful buildings that line the waterways.

Brugge's unique location in the Flanders region of Belgium means that it is centrally placed for exploring both the countryside and nearby cities. It is easily accessible by train from Brussels and other major Belgian cities, and it is a great base for day trips to places like Ghent and the Belgian coastline.

Culturally, Brugge is renowned for its art and history. The city was a major center of the medieval world, serving as a hub for trade, especially during the 12th and 13th centuries. Over time, Brugge became a significant part of European cultural and economic life, and its importance is reflected in the art and architecture that define it today. In 2025, Brugge continues to be a place where history meets modern-day living, with its streets lined with art galleries, cafes, and independent shops that add a fresh, local flair to the old-world atmosphere.

For tourists, Brugge offers a delightful blend of history, culture, and modernity. Whether you're exploring its medieval museums, wandering the cobbled streets, or enjoying a quiet moment at one of the city's famous squares, Brugge has something for everyone. It's a place where you can step back in time while still enjoying modern comforts and experiences.

A Brief History of Brugge

Brugge's history is one of wealth, power, and influence. During the Middle Ages, Brugge was one of the wealthiest cities in Europe. Its location along key trade routes allowed it to flourish as a center for commerce, especially with the Hanseatic League, a powerful network of cities that controlled trade in Northern Europe. Brugge was known for its textiles and cloth production, which made it one of the most important cities in the medieval world.

By the 12th century, Brugge had become a major trading hub. The city's position along the waterways made it the perfect place for merchants from across Europe to converge. In fact, Brugge's success in trade during this time earned it the nickname "Venice of the North." The city was also a major cultural center, attracting artists, philosophers, and scholars, and it became home to many important guilds and institutions.

In the 15th century, Brugge reached the height of its power and wealth. However, the city's prosperity began to decline in the 16th century due to changes in trade routes and political shifts. By the 18th century, Brugge had become somewhat isolated, and much of its influence faded. The city went through a long period of stagnation, but this allowed its medieval architecture and charm to remain relatively intact.

In the 19th century, Brugge's fortunes turned around. The city began to attract tourists interested in its historic beauty and medieval past. In 2000, Brugge was designated a UNESCO World Heritage site, ensuring its preservation for future generations. Today, the city's rich history is on full display, with museums, historical buildings, and landmarks telling the story of its rise and fall.

As of 2025, Brugge's past is still very much alive in its streets, squares, and canals. Visitors can experience what life was like during the city's medieval heyday by touring its historic buildings, museums, and monuments. The Belfry of Brugge, which dates back to the 13th century, still stands tall in the heart of the city, offering panoramic views of the city's charming rooftops and canals. Other iconic landmarks, such as the Church of Our Lady and the Basilica of the Holy Blood, provide glimpses into Brugge's past and its importance as a religious center.

Why Visit Brugge in 2025?

Brugge in 2025 offers visitors a rich blend of history, art, and modernity. The city has managed to preserve its historic charm while also embracing modern developments that enhance the visitor experience. For example, the city's focus on sustainability has led to improvements in eco-friendly transport options, including bike rentals and electric vehicle charging stations. Brugge's canals, which have been central to the city's identity for centuries, are still as picturesque as ever, but they have been made more accessible with boat tours that offer a relaxed way to explore the city's waterways.

In 2025, Brugge is more vibrant than ever. The city's lively arts scene continues to thrive, with new galleries and art exhibitions popping up regularly. There's also a growing food scene, with local chefs embracing traditional Belgian cuisine while adding their own innovative twists. Brugge's festivals and events in 2025 continue to draw crowds from all over the world. The city's famous Procession of the Holy Blood, a religious festival that takes place every year in May, is a major highlight, with a parade that features beautiful floats, costumes, and religious rituals.

For those interested in Belgian culture, Brugge offers some of the best museums and galleries in the country. The Groeningemuseum, which houses an impressive collection of Flemish Primitive paintings, is a must-visit for art lovers. Additionally, the city's focus on local craftmanship, especially lace-making and chocolate production, makes it an ideal destination for those looking to experience authentic Belgian traditions.

Brugge also continues to be an accessible city for tourists, with improvements to public transportation and a wide range of activities for all interests. Whether you want to explore its rich history, enjoy its natural beauty, or indulge in its growing culinary scene, Brugge in 2025 is a place that caters to all types of travelers.

What's New in Brugge for 2025?

Brugge is always evolving, and 2025 brings some exciting new developments for tourists. The city has embraced its role as a leading cultural destination with the opening of several new attractions and spaces.

One of the most exciting additions to the city in 2025 is the opening of the *Brugge Art & Culture Center*, located near the historic center. This modern venue is dedicated to showcasing contemporary art while respecting the city's historic character. Visitors can expect rotating exhibitions featuring both Belgian and international artists, with a focus on local talent. The center also offers a range of cultural events, including concerts, theater performances, and workshops for all ages. It's an excellent place for art lovers to experience Brugge's evolving creative scene.

Additionally, Brugge's food scene has seen a transformation in recent years, with several new, trendy restaurants opening in the city. *The Tasting Room*, a modern Belgian restaurant offering a tasting menu featuring seasonal ingredients and local Belgian wines, is one of the highlights. It's located just a short walk from the Markt Square and offers a modern take on traditional Flemish dishes, providing visitors with a fresh dining experience.

For those interested in outdoor activities, Brugge has made improvements to its bike paths and walking trails. The new *Brugge Cycling Route* connects the city center with nearby villages, providing visitors with an easy way to explore the countryside and experience the beauty of the region's canals and farmland. The city has also invested in new eco-friendly boats for canal tours, allowing tourists to explore Brugge's waterways in a more sustainable way.

Finally, the city's hotel scene is also evolving. *Hotel De Orangerie*, a beautiful boutique hotel located near the canal, has undergone a major renovation in 2025, making it one of the most luxurious and sought-after places to stay in Brugge. With its elegant rooms, stunning views of the canal, and prime location, it's a top choice for visitors looking for a stylish and comfortable stay.

In addition to these developments, Brugge is also home to several exciting festivals and events in 2025, including a new culinary festival focused on Belgian beer and food pairing, which is expected to attract food lovers from all over the world.

Essential Travel Tips

Best Time to Visit Brugge

Brugge is a city that can be enjoyed year-round, but the best time to visit depends on what kind of experience you're after. The seasonal appeal of Brugge varies, so here's a breakdown of what to expect during each season.

Spring (March to May):

Spring is a wonderful time to visit Brugge. The weather begins to warm up, with average temperatures ranging from 7°C (45°F) to 15°C (59°F). This is the season when the city starts to come alive with flowers blooming and outdoor cafes filling up. Early spring, especially March and April, is a great time to avoid large crowds while still enjoying pleasant weather. This time of year also sees the start of the tourist season, so there are fewer tourists around, giving you a more relaxed experience when visiting top attractions like the Belfry Tower or the Markt Square.

In late spring, around May, the crowds start to pick up a bit as the weather gets warmer, but it's still far from the peak summer rush. If you're visiting for the flowers and the fresh spring air, Brugge is at its best in April and May.

Summer (June to August):

Summer is the busiest time in Brugge, especially from June to August, when the city is packed with tourists. The weather is generally pleasant, with average temperatures ranging from 15°C (59°F) to 21°C (70°F). It's the perfect time to enjoy Brugge's outdoor activities, like boat tours along the canals or a stroll through the historic center. The streets and main attractions can get crowded during this time, and accommodation prices may be higher due to the influx of visitors.

If you don't mind the crowds and are keen on experiencing the city at its liveliest, then summer is the right choice. You'll find that outdoor cafes and restaurants are bustling, and there are many festivals and events happening, like the annual Procession of the Holy Blood in May. However, it's important to note that this is when Brugge sees its highest number of tourists, so be prepared for long lines and crowded spaces.

Fall (September to November):

Fall is arguably the best time to visit Brugge for a more peaceful experience. The weather remains mild through September and October, with average temperatures ranging from 10°C (50°F) to 15°C (59°F), though it can get cooler as November approaches. September and October are perfect for those who want to enjoy Brugge's outdoor attractions without the overwhelming crowds that summer brings. You'll still experience pleasant weather, and the fall foliage along the canals adds a beautiful touch to the city's already scenic landscape.

In addition, Brugge hosts several festivals and events during the fall, including the Film Fest Gent in October, which is just a short train ride away if you're looking for something more exciting outside of the city.

By November, the weather can get chillier, and you'll see fewer tourists, but it's still a great time to enjoy the quieter atmosphere. Be sure to pack a warm jacket if you're visiting this time of year.

Winter (December to February):

Winter in Brugge is magical, especially during the holiday season. The city transforms into a winter wonderland, with Christmas markets popping up and the cobblestone streets lit up with festive decorations. December is the peak of the winter season, with average temperatures around 3°C (37°F), so it's cold, but it's still manageable if you bundle up. This is when you can enjoy Brugge's cozy atmosphere, with warm drinks and local delicacies like Belgian waffles and hot chocolate.

However, winter can be quiet in Brugge, with fewer tourists visiting compared to other times of the year. Many shops and restaurants close early, but the beauty of Brugge covered in snow is worth it. If you don't mind the cold and prefer avoiding crowds, winter offers a peaceful yet picturesque view of the city.

Tips for Avoiding Peak Tourist Season:

To avoid the busy summer months while still experiencing Brugge at its best, the best time to visit would be late spring (April to May) or early fall (September to early October). During these months, you'll find the weather enjoyable, the crowds manageable, and the prices lower. You can still enjoy all the attractions and activities, but without the long lines and inflated costs.

Currency and Local Customs

Belgium uses the Euro (€) as its official currency. Most places in Brugge accept credit cards, but it's always a good idea to carry some cash for smaller purchases or in case you visit a more traditional shop. You can find ATMs around the city center where you can withdraw cash, and currency exchange services are available if needed, although they may charge a fee. Major banks and post offices in Brugge offer currency exchange as well. Here's what you need to know about currency and customs in Brugge.

Tipping Practices in Brugge:

Tipping in Belgium is not mandatory, but it is appreciated, especially if you're happy with the service. In restaurants, a service charge is often included in your bill, but it's still customary to leave a small tip of around 5-10% for good service. For example, if your meal costs €50, leaving a tip of €2-€5 is typical.

In cafes or bars, if you're just having a drink, rounding up the bill is common. For instance, if your coffee costs €2.50, rounding it up to €3 is a simple and appreciated gesture. In taxis, rounding the fare to the nearest euro or adding a couple of extra euros is also customary, but not required.

For hotel staff, such as bellhops or housekeepers, tips are appreciated but not expected. A couple of euros for good service is a polite way to show gratitude. For example, €1-€2 per day for housekeeping is a good guideline.

How Locals Greet Each Other:

Belgians are generally polite and formal when greeting others. A simple "Hallo" or "Goedemorgen" (Good morning) is common when you meet someone. If you're meeting someone in a more formal setting or for the first time, you may want to shake hands. It's also customary to greet people with a "kissing" gesture in more informal settings, but this is typically only between friends or close acquaintances, and usually involves two or three kisses on the cheek.

When addressing people, it's polite to use their titles if you know them (e.g.,

Mr., Mrs., Doctor) unless you've been invited to use first names. If in doubt, it's best to be formal at first and then gauge whether it's appropriate to switch to a more casual tone.

Local Etiquette to Keep in Mind:

1. Punctuality: Belgians value punctuality, so make sure you're on time for any appointments, whether it's a tour, dinner reservation, or meeting a friend.

2. Quiet Public Spaces: While the city of Brugge is busy with tourists, locals tend to be respectful of public spaces. Be mindful of your noise level, especially in cafes or public transport.

3. Respect for Personal Space: Personal space is important, so avoid standing too close to others, especially in crowded places like elevators or public transport.

4. Dress Code: Belgians generally dress well but not overly formal. Casual attire is perfectly acceptable for most tourist attractions, but you may want to dress a bit nicer when dining in higher-end restaurants.

Key Cultural Notes:

- **Belgian Beer**: Beer is an integral part of Belgian culture. When visiting a local pub or bar, it's polite to ask for recommendations. Belgium is home to over 1,000 different types of beer, so take the time to try some varieties.
- **Language**: The main language spoken in Brugge is Flemish (a variant of Dutch), but most people speak English, especially in the city center and tourist areas. It's always appreciated if you can greet people with a simple "Hallo" or "Dank u wel" (Thank you).

Where to Exchange Currency

While Brugge has several places to exchange currency, here are the best options:

1. Bank of Brussels (Belfortstraat 1, 8000 Brugge): Located in the city center, this is a reliable place to exchange currency. They offer competitive exchange rates.

2. Post Office (Mariastraat 34, 8000 Brugge): Another option for currency exchange and a trusted institution for withdrawing euros.

3. ATMs: ATMs are widely available throughout the city. The machine on Markt Square is one of the most centrally located and convenient options.

Language and Communication Tips

In Brugge, the primary language spoken is Dutch, also known locally as Flemish. However, because Brugge is a popular tourist destination, English is widely spoken, especially in areas frequented by visitors. This means that most people working in tourist spots, such as shops, cafes, museums, and hotels, will be able to communicate with you in English. However, knowing a few basic phrases in Dutch/Flemish can enhance your experience and show respect for the local culture.

The Language Situation in Brugge

Flemish is essentially the Belgian variety of Dutch, and it is spoken by the majority of the population in the Flanders region, where Brugge is located. While it shares many similarities with standard Dutch, Flemish can have slight differences in pronunciation and vocabulary. The written language is nearly identical to Dutch, so if you can read Dutch, you will find it easy to navigate in Brugge.

Even though most locals speak Flemish, you will find that the younger generations and those working in tourism are comfortable with English. In fact, English is taught in schools from an early age, and many people are proficient. However, it's always appreciated when visitors make an effort to learn a few key phrases in the local language.

Practical Tips for Communication

While English is common, not everyone in Brugge will speak it fluently, especially in more rural areas or when dealing with older locals. In these cases, speaking a bit of Flemish can be helpful, and even just a simple "Hallo" (Hello) or "Dank u wel" (Thank you) can go a long way. Locals will appreciate your effort to speak their language, even if it's just a few words.

1. Speak Slowly and Clearly:

When speaking English, it's best to speak slowly and clearly, especially when addressing someone who may not be a native English speaker. Keep sentences simple, and avoid complex vocabulary or idiomatic expressions that may be difficult to understand.

2. Be Polite and Respectful:

In Brugge, like the rest of Belgium, politeness is important. People often greet one another formally, especially in business settings. Using a friendly but respectful tone will help create positive interactions.

Useful Phrases in Dutch/Flemish

Here is a list of essential phrases that will come in handy during your visit to Brugge. Knowing these phrases will help you in daily interactions, whether you're ordering food, asking for directions, or simply greeting people.

LANGUAGE AND COMMUNICATION TIPS

Greetings and Polite Phrases:

- **Hallo** (HAH-lo) – Hello
- **Goedemorgen** (GOO-duh-mor-ghen) – Good morning
- **Goedenavond** (GOO-duh-naah-vond) – Good evening
- **Goedenacht** (GOO-duh-nacht) – Good night
- **Hoe gaat het?** (Hoo gaat ut?) – How are you?
- **Het gaat goed, dank je wel.** (Ut gaat hood, dank yuh vel) – I'm good, thank you.
- **Wat is je naam?** (Vah t iss yuh nahm?) – What is your name?
- **Mijn naam is [name].** (Mine nahm is [name]) – My name is [name].
- **Prettige dag!** (PRET-tuh-he dahkh) – Have a nice day!
- **Tot ziens!** (Tot zeens) – See you later!
- **Alstublieft** (AHL-stu-bleeft) – Please (formal)
- **Dank u wel** (Dank u vel) – Thank you (formal)
- **Dank je wel** (Dank yuh vel) – Thank you (informal)
- **Sorry!** (SOR-ee) – Sorry!

Common Phrases for Shopping, Eating, and Ordering Food:

- **Hoeveel kost dit?** (How much is this?)
- **Mag ik de rekening, alstublieft?** (May I have the bill, please?)
- **Heeft u een menukaart?** (Do you have a menu?)
- **Mag ik de kaart alstublieft?** (Can I have the menu please?)
- **Ik wil graag [item].** (I would like [item].)
- **Wat raad u aan?** (What do you recommend?)
- **Ik ben vegetariër.** (I'm a vegetarian.)
- **Hebt u iets zonder vlees?** (Do you have something without meat?)
- **Ik ben allergisch voor [item].** (I'm allergic to [item].)
- **Mag ik wat water?** (Can I have some water?)
- **Een biertje alstublieft.** (A beer please.)
- **Heeft u Wi-Fi?** (Do you have Wi-Fi?)

Asking for Directions:

- **Waar is [location]?** (Where is [location]?)
- **Hoe kom ik bij [location]?** (How do I get to [location]?)
- **Is het ver van hier?** (Is it far from here?)
- **Hoe ver is het naar het station?** (How far is it to the station?)
- **Rechtdoor** (Straight ahead)
- **Links** (Left)
- **Rechts** (Right)
- **Stop hier, alstublieft.** (Stop here, please.)
- **Is het ver lopen?** (Is it far to walk?)
- **Kunt u mij helpen?** (Can you help me?)

Emergency and Helpful Phrases:

- **Ik heb hulp nodig.** (I need help.)
- **Waar is het ziekenhuis?** (Where is the hospital?)
- **Bel 112!** (Call 112 – Emergency number)
- **Ik ben verloren.** (I am lost.)
- **Mag ik een taxi bellen?** (Can I call a taxi?)
- **Ik heb mijn paspoort verloren.** (I have lost my passport.)

Important Notes on Pronunciation: While Dutch/Flemish pronunciation can be tricky, here are some tips to help you sound more natural:

- **"J"** is pronounced like "Y" in English. For example, "Dank je wel" sounds like "Dank yuh vel."
- **"G"** is pronounced as a guttural sound, similar to clearing your throat. It's a sound that doesn't exist in English, but it's important for words like "goed" (good) or "goedenacht" (good night).
- **"Sch"** sounds like "skh," similar to the beginning of "scoot." For example,

"school" (school) is pronounced "skhool."

Using Basic English

While English is widely spoken in Brugge, there are some situations where you may need to speak a bit more clearly or slow down your speech. Most people in Brugge working in tourist areas are fluent in English, but in small shops or places less frequented by tourists, it's polite to start with a greeting in Dutch or Flemish, like "Hallo" or "Goedemorgen." If you start by speaking in Dutch/Flemish, locals will often switch to English if they sense you're not familiar with the language.

When asking for directions, most people will respond in a combination of Dutch and English, or they'll switch to English if they understand you better. As in many European cities, younger people are typically more comfortable speaking English, while older generations may not be as fluent.

Language Etiquette

In Brugge, like much of Belgium, it's important to be polite and respectful. When speaking to someone, always use "alstublieft" (please) and "dank u wel" (thank you) in formal situations. These small gestures will show respect for the local customs, and in return, you'll be greeted with warmth and friendliness.

When addressing someone formally, use "u" for "you" rather than "je" or "jij" (informal "you"). This is a sign of respect and is important when speaking to strangers or in professional settings.

Cultural Considerations

While the Flemish language is widely spoken, you'll also hear French and English, especially in areas near the border or in tourist-heavy spots. The knowledge of multiple languages is very common among the locals, so don't hesitate to ask if you need help.

In restaurants, cafes, or shops, locals expect polite and simple interactions. It's perfectly fine to start with "Excuseer" (excuse me) if you're approaching someone, especially if you're interrupting their conversation or their work.

Final Tips

- **Be patient**: If you're trying out Flemish or Dutch phrases, locals appreciate the effort but may switch to English if they feel it will be easier.

- **Use gestures**: If you don't know a specific phrase or word, don't be afraid to use hand gestures or point. Most people will understand and try to help.

By picking up a few simple phrases and being mindful of local customs, you'll have a more pleasant and respectful experience in Brugge. The effort you put into speaking Flemish will be appreciated, and you'll likely find that it opens up more friendly interactions with the locals.

Safety Tips and Essential Resources

Safety Tips and Local Etiquette

Brugge is a safe city for tourists, but as with any popular travel destination, it's important to stay aware of your surroundings. Here are some safety tips and local etiquette to help you have a smooth and secure visit.

Personal Security: Brugge is known for its low crime rate, but pickpocketing can occur, especially in busy tourist areas like Market Square (Markt) or near the Belfry Tower. Here's how to stay safe:

- **Keep valuables close**: Avoid carrying large amounts of cash, and always keep your wallet, phone, and passport in a secure place, such as a front pocket or a money belt.

- **Be cautious in crowded areas**: Tourists often become targets for pickpockets in crowded spaces. Be extra vigilant when you're in lines, on public transport, or at popular attractions.

- **Use a hotel safe**: If your accommodation offers a safe, use it to store valuable items that you don't need to carry with you.

- **Avoid isolated areas after dark**: Brugge's historic center is quite safe, but like any city, it's best to avoid poorly lit or isolated areas late at night, especially if you're alone.

- **Taxi safety**: If you need a taxi, it's best to call one through a reputable service or ask your hotel to arrange it for you. Always make sure the taxi is registered.

Dealing with Pickpockets:

- **Be aware of common tactics**: Pickpockets often work in teams, using distractions like asking for directions or bumping into you to make a quick grab. Be mindful of anyone getting too close, and don't hesitate to move away if you feel uncomfortable.

- **Keep an eye on your belongings**: When sitting at outdoor cafes or in busy public areas, make sure your bags are closed and that you keep your belongings within sight.

General Local Etiquette:

- **Greetings**: Belgians tend to greet each other with a handshake or a friendly "Hallo" (Hello). In informal settings, people may greet with a kiss on both cheeks, but this is usually reserved for close friends or family.

- **Queueing**: Belgians are generally polite and respectful in public spaces, so always queue for services, such as at bus stops or in shops.

- **Dress code**: The dress code in Brugge is casual but neat. If you're visiting a religious site, it's respectful to dress modestly. While shorts are fine in the summer, sleeveless tops may be frowned upon in certain churches or museums.

- **Tipping**: Tipping is not mandatory in Belgium, but it's appreciated. In restaurants, a service charge is often included in the bill, but if it's not, you can leave a tip of about 5-10%. In cafes or bars, rounding up the bill or leaving a small tip is common.

- **Respectful behavior**: Be mindful of personal space in Brugge. Belgians appreciate their privacy, so avoid being overly loud in public or invading someone's personal space.

Health and Emergency Information

Access to Medical Care: Brugge has a good standard of healthcare, with several hospitals, clinics, and pharmacies available for both emergencies and general medical needs.

Hospitals:

(I) AZ Sint-Jan Brugge-Oostende (Sint-Jan Hospital)

- Address: Brieversstraat 6, 8000 Brugge, Belgium
- Phone: +32 50 45 23 11
- This is the main hospital in Brugge, offering emergency care and general medical services.

(ii) AZ Sint-Lucas Hospital

- Address: Ruddershove 10, 8000 Brugge, Belgium
- Phone: +32 50 45 73 00
- Another hospital option if you require urgent medical attention or specialized care.

Pharmacies: Pharmacies in Brugge are easy to find, especially in the city center. If you need medicine or have a health issue, you can visit any pharmacy, where they'll offer advice or refer you to a doctor if necessary. Some well-known pharmacies are:

(I) Apotheek van der Weijden

- Address: Sint-Jakobsstraat 26, 8000 Brugge
- Phone: +32 50 33 06 88
- **Apotheek Swaenenburg**
- Address: Walplein 5, 8000 Brugge
- Phone: +32 50 34 03 61

Emergency Numbers: In case of an emergency, it's important to know the local emergency numbers. Here's what you'll need:

(I) Emergency Services (Police, Fire, Ambulance): 112

- This is the universal emergency number in Belgium for police, fire, and medical emergencies. It's free of charge and can be dialed from any phone, including mobile phones.

(ii) Poison Control: +32 70 245 245

- If you or someone you know has been poisoned, this is the number to call for immediate assistance.

Health Risks and Vaccination

Suggestions: Brugge does not have any major health risks that would concern travelers. However, it's always good to check if you're up to date on routine vaccinations such as measles, mumps, rubella (MMR), diphtheria, tetanus, and pertussis.

COVID-19: As of 2025, Belgium has largely returned to pre-pandemic normalcy, but travelers should still be aware of local health guidelines regarding COVID-19, especially in crowded areas or on public transport.

Flu Season: Flu is common in the colder months (October to March). If you're visiting during this time, be sure to wash your hands regularly and avoid close contact with people showing symptoms.

Useful Apps and Resources

When traveling to Brugge, several apps and websites can help make your visit smoother and more enjoyable. Whether you're navigating the city, finding a restaurant, or booking tickets for attractions, here are some essential resources.

Transportation and Navigation:

(I) Google Maps: A must-have for navigating Brugge's streets and canals. It provides walking directions and information on public transportation routes, helping you get around easily.

(ii) SNCB (Belgian National Railway): For train travel, use the SNCB app to check schedules and purchase tickets for trips to and from Brugge. This is especially helpful if you're planning to explore surrounding cities like Ghent or Brussels.

App available for iOS and Android.

(I) De Lijn: Brugge's bus service is managed by De Lijn. This app provides bus schedules, routes, and real-time updates. It's helpful for getting around Brugge and beyond, particularly to nearby areas like the Belgian coast.

Finding Restaurants and Things to Do:

(I) TripAdvisor: For finding up-to-date restaurant recommendations, things to do, and reviews, TripAdvisor is a reliable resource. While Brugge has many excellent options, TripAdvisor helps you find the most recent and recommended places based on user feedback.

(ii) Yelp: Another great app for exploring the best dining options in Brugge, from traditional Belgian meals to international cuisine. It also includes reviews for activities and shops.

(iii) Visit Brugge (official tourism website): Visit the official tourism website of Brugge to get the latest information on events, festivals, museum openings, and any important local news. Website: www.visitbruges.be

Language and Communication:

- **Google Translate**: While many people in Brugge speak English, it's still useful to have Google Translate on hand in case you want to look up specific phrases or read menus in Flemish. The app can be used offline and translates text in real-time using your camera.

Staying Connected:

- **Wi-Fi Map**: If you need Wi-Fi access during your trip, Wi-Fi Map can help you find free public Wi-Fi hotspots in Brugge. The app also provides details on passwords for cafes and other public areas that offer Wi-Fi.

Local Services and Emergency Help:

- **112 BE**: This is an emergency services app that provides quick access to emergency numbers in Belgium. It allows you to directly dial emergency services such as the police, fire department, or ambulance.
- **Emergency+**: This app is particularly useful if you find yourself in an emergency and need to know your location. It uses GPS to provide emergency services with your exact position, which can be crucial in critical situations.

Final Advice

When traveling to Brugge, it's important to stay aware of your surroundings, especially in crowded places. Don't hesitate to use the emergency services number 112 if you need assistance. For health-related concerns, the hospitals and pharmacies in Brugge provide excellent services. To make your trip easier, make use of travel apps that help with navigation, booking activities, and finding useful services.

Getting to Brugge

Arriving by Plane

Brugge does not have its own airport, but it is well-served by several major airports in Belgium and neighboring countries. The two most common airports for travelers flying into Brugge are **Brussels Airport** (Zaventem) and **Oostende-Brugge International Airport**.

1. Brussels Airport (Zaventem)

- **Address**: Brussels Airport, 1930 Zaventem, Belgium
- **Website**: www.brusselsairport.be
- **Distance to Brugge**: Approximately 100 km (62 miles)
- **Travel Time to Brugge**: About 1 hour 30 minutes by car or public transport.

Brussels Airport is the main international gateway to Belgium, handling flights from around the world. It is located around 100 kilometers southeast of Brugge, and it's very well connected to the city via public transport and taxis. Here's how to get from Brussels Airport to Brugge:

By Train: The most convenient way to travel from Brussels Airport to Brugge is by train. Trains to Brugge leave frequently from **Brussels Airport Railway Station** (located under the airport). Trains usually depart every 30 minutes and take about **1 hour** and **10 minutes** to reach Brugge Central Station.

- **Cost**: A one-way ticket costs around €15.
- **Ticket purchase**: You can buy tickets at the self-service machines or counters at the train station inside the airport. Tickets are also available online through the SNCB (Belgian National Railway) website or app.
- **Direct or transfer trains**: Some trains go directly to Brugge, while others require a transfer at **Brussels Central Station** or **Antwerp Central Station**. Make sure to check your schedule for the best option.
- **Travel Tip**: Trains in Belgium are punctual, but it's always a good idea to check live schedules for any delays on the official SNCB website or app.

By Taxi: Taxis are available outside the arrivals terminal at Brussels Airport. A taxi ride to Brugge will take about **1 hour 30 minutes**, depending on traffic.

- **Cost**: The fare is typically between **€130 and €160**, depending on traffic and time of day.
- **Booking**: You can either hop in a taxi at the airport or pre-book one using a local taxi service or app. It's recommended to confirm the fare with the driver before starting the journey.
- **Travel Tip**: Taxis can be a convenient option if you have heavy luggage or are traveling in a group, but it is more expensive than the train.

By Shuttle: Several shuttle services run from Brussels Airport to Brugge. These services are usually pre-booked and can take you directly from the airport to your accommodation or other designated locations in Brugge.

- **Cost**: Shuttle prices can vary, but expect to pay around **€25 to €35 per person** for a shared ride. Private shuttle services can cost more, generally around **€100** or more.
- **Travel Tip**: If you're traveling with a group or family, a private shuttle

may offer better value.

2. Oostende-Brugge International Airport

- **Address**: Ostend-Bruges International Airport, 8400 Oostende, Belgium
- **Website**: www.ostendairport.be
- **Distance to Brugge:** About 30 km (19 miles)
- **Travel Time to Brugge**: Approximately 30 minutes by car or taxi, or 40 minutes by public transport.

Oostende-Brugge International Airport is a smaller regional airport but still serves both international and European flights. It's located closer to Brugge than Brussels Airport and offers a quick and convenient journey into the city.

By Taxi: Taxis are available at the airport and are the most direct way to get to Brugge from Oostende-Brugge Airport.

- **Cost**: A taxi ride costs around **€40 to €50** for a one-way trip.
- **Travel Tip**: Always check with the driver about the fare before beginning your trip to avoid surprises.

By Public Transport: Public transport options from Oostende-Brugge Airport to Brugge are quite simple. First, you will need to take a bus from the airport to **Oostende Railway Station**, which takes about **10 minutes**. From there, you can take a direct train to Brugge.

- **Total Travel Time**: Around **40 minutes**.
- **Cost**: The total cost is usually around **€6 to €8** for a one-way ticket.
- **Travel Tip**: Trains from Oostende to Brugge depart every 15 to 30 minutes, so it's an easy connection.

Arriving by Train

Brugge is well-connected by train to many major cities in Belgium and beyond. The **Brugge Central Railway Station** is the main train station in the city and is located just a short walk from the city center. It's an ideal starting point for your trip, whether you're coming from within Belgium or arriving from neighboring countries.

From Brussels to Brugge

Trains between Brussels and Brugge run frequently throughout the day. The journey from **Brussels Central Station** to **Brugge Central Station** takes around **1 hour** and **10 minutes**.

- **Cost**: A one-way ticket from Brussels to Brugge typically costs around **€15**.
- **Train Types**: There are direct trains available, as well as options with one transfer at Brussels-South or another major hub.
- **Ticket purchase**: You can buy tickets at Brussels Central Station, from vending machines, or online via the **SNCB** app or website.
- **Travel Tip**: If you're traveling during rush hour (weekdays from 7 AM to 9 AM or 5 PM to 7 PM), be prepared for more crowded trains. Consider purchasing tickets in advance to ensure a seat.

From Ghent to Brugge

If you're coming from **Ghent**, it's a short ride to Brugge, and the trains depart frequently from **Gent-Sint-Pieters Station** to **Brugge Central Station**.

- **Travel Time**: The journey takes approximately **25 to 30 minutes**.

- **Cost**: A one-way ticket is around €5.
- **Train Types**: There are direct trains available, so this is an easy route to take.
- **Ticket purchase**: Tickets can be purchased at the station, online, or through the SNCB app.
- **Travel Tip**: This is one of the easiest and quickest ways to get to Brugge from another Belgian city, especially if you're already in Ghent. Trains run every 30 minutes.

From Other Major Cities

- **Antwerp to Brugge**: Trains from Antwerp's **Antwerp Central Station** to Brugge take about **1 hour 10 minutes**. The cost is typically **€15**.
- **Brussels Airport to Brugge**: As mentioned above, you can take a train directly from **Brussels Airport** to Brugge. The journey takes around **1 hour 10 minutes**.
- **Lille (France) to Brugge**: If you're traveling from France, you can catch a direct **TGV** train from Lille to Brugge. The journey takes around **1 hour 30 minutes**. The cost is around **€20 to €30**.

Additional Train Travel Tips

- **Tickets**: Tickets for trains can be purchased at the station, online, or via the SNCB app. For tickets purchased at the station, be sure to check the price on the digital displays to confirm you're buying the right one. For longer journeys, it's worth purchasing in advance to secure the best price.

- **SNCB App**: The SNCB app is very useful for checking schedules, buying tickets, and checking real-time updates for your journey. It's available for both Android and iOS.

- **Luggage**: Trains in Belgium typically have space for luggage, but it's always a good idea to keep your bags close to you in the designated luggage areas or under your seat.

- **Seat Reservations**: For most domestic trains in Belgium, seat reservations are not required. However, if you are traveling during busy periods or to/from major cities, it's always a good idea to arrive early and grab a seat, especially on express trains.

Other Considerations for Train Travel

- **Accessibility**: Brugge Central Station is equipped with facilities for travelers with reduced mobility, including ramps, elevators, and assistance services. If you need assistance, it's a good idea to contact the station ahead of time.

- **Travel Passes**: If you plan to travel to several cities in Belgium, consider purchasing a **Go Pass** or a **Belgian Rail Pass**, which offers unlimited train travel for a set number of days.

- **Travel Tip**: Make sure to check your schedule before traveling, as there may be occasional delays or changes to train times.

Navigating Brugge

How to Get Around the City

Brugge is a compact city, making it relatively easy to get around, whether you're walking, cycling, or using public transport. The city's well-preserved medieval layout means most attractions are within walking distance of each other, but if you prefer public transport or cycling, Brugge has a range of options to help you navigate efficiently.

Walking in Brugge

The best way to explore Brugge is on foot. The historic city center is filled with narrow streets, charming canals, and picturesque squares, all of which are best discovered at a slow pace. Walking allows you to fully take in the beauty of Brugge's architecture and its peaceful atmosphere. Most of the city's main attractions, like the Belfry, Markt Square, and the Basilica of the Holy Blood, are just a short walk away from each other.

Travel Tip: Bring comfortable shoes, as you'll be walking on cobblestone streets, which can be uneven at times.

Best Walking Routes: The city's main walking routes are well-marked with signs, and several walking tours are available if you want a guided experience.

Popular routes include the canal-side path from the Minnewater (Lake of Love) to the city center, and the route that loops around the historic center with stops at all the major landmarks.

Cycling Around Brugge

Cycling is another excellent way to get around Brugge. The city is known for its bike-friendly atmosphere, with many dedicated bike lanes and paths. Brugge is relatively flat, making it easy to explore on two wheels. It's also an eco-friendly option, as Brugge promotes sustainable travel.

Bike Rental: Renting a bike is simple. There are several rental shops in the city center where you can get a bike for the day or longer. Some options include:

(I) Brugge Bike Rental

- Address: Molenbeekpark 1, 8000 Brugge
- Contact: +32 50 34 62 75
- Cost: Around €10-€15 per day for a standard bike. Electric bikes are available for around €20 per day.

(ii) Fietsen De Vijfhoek

- Address: Korte Vuldersstraat 24, 8000 Brugge
- Contact: +32 50 34 52 53
- Cost: Bikes for rent starting at €12 per day.
- **Travel Tip**: If you plan to use a bike for several days, check if the rental shop offers discounts for multiple-day rentals.

Cycling Routes in Brugge

Brugge is one of the most scenic cities to explore by bike. The network of canals and green spaces makes cycling a delightful way to see the city. Here are some of the best cycling routes:

The Canal Route: This route takes you along Brugge's main canals, passing through some of the city's most picturesque and quieter areas. Start at the **Minnewater** (Lake of Love), and cycle along the **Begijnhof** and **Dijver Canal**, reaching as far as the **Ezelstraat** area. This is a leisurely route and perfect for sightseeing.

The Cycle Route to Damme: For those who want to venture beyond the city, you can follow the bike path from Brugge to **Damme**, a charming town about 7 km (4 miles) away. This route takes you through open fields and quiet countryside, giving you a real taste of the Flemish landscape.

The Green Belt Route: A scenic route that connects the outer parts of Brugge, looping through local parks and green spaces. It's a bit longer, ideal for cyclists who want a relaxing ride that also allows them to escape the hustle and bustle of the city center.

Travel Tip: Keep an eye on your bike rental shop's return policy, as some bikes need to be returned by a specific time or day, and late fees may apply.

Public Transport: Buses and Trams

While walking and cycling are often the best ways to explore Brugge, there are also public transport options available, particularly for those who want to explore more of the region or need to travel further afield.

Buses: Brugge has an efficient and affordable bus network, operated by **De Lijn**, which can take you to places within and around the city. The buses are well-maintained, and there are plenty of routes connecting the city center with neighborhoods, suburbs, and other nearby towns.

Ticket Information:

A single bus ticket costs about €3 for a journey within the city. If you're planning to take multiple bus rides, you can purchase a **Day Pass** for around €7, which offers unlimited travel within the Brugge region for one day.

Key Routes:

Bus 3: This bus travels from **Brugge Central Station** to **Sint-Kruis**, a nearby district.

Bus 11: This route connects Brugge with **Oostende**, making it useful for those traveling to the Belgian coast.

Bus 12: This goes to the **Bruges Railway Station** (station) and takes visitors to nearby neighborhoods such as **Eeklo** and **Zeebrugge**.

Travel Tip: If you're staying for a few days and plan on using public transport frequently, consider purchasing a **De Lijn pass** that offers unlimited travel on buses throughout the Brugge area.

Trams: While Brugge itself does not have an extensive tram system, there is a tram line running from Brugge to **Oostende**, located about 30 kilometers away. The tram ride provides an opportunity to see more of the Flemish countryside and coastal areas. The tram also connects Brugge with the towns along the Belgian coast, including **Blankenberge** and **Zeebrugge**.

Ticket Information:

A single tram ticket from Brugge to **Oostende** costs around €5, while a return ticket will cost approximately **€9**.

Travel Tip: Trams are a good option if you're heading to the coast for a day trip, but they aren't necessary for navigating Brugge itself, as most attractions are walkable.

Taxis and Ride-Sharing

Though Brugge is small and easy to navigate by foot or bike, taxis are available for those who prefer a more private and direct option. You'll find taxis waiting outside major stations like **Brugge Central Station** and **Market Square**.

- **Cost**: A typical taxi fare from Brugge's city center to nearby areas is around €10-€15. Prices can increase depending on the distance and time of day.
- **Ride-sharing Apps**: While **Uber** is not available in Brugge, other local ride-sharing apps like **Bolt** operate in the area. Prices are similar to those of traditional taxis, and it's a convenient option if you prefer to book a ride via your phone.

Car Rentals

Although Brugge is compact and walkable, some visitors might prefer the flexibility of a rental car, especially if they plan to explore beyond the city. Car rental services are available at **Brugge Central Station** or nearby locations.

- **Cost**: Daily rental prices for a small car start at around **€40 to €50**, depending on the season and rental company. If you're only visiting Brugge and not planning to travel outside the city, renting a car might not be necessary, as public transport and bikes are much more practical.
- **Parking**: Parking in Brugge's city center can be tricky and expensive. Parking is available at various spots around the city, but be prepared to pay between **€2 to €3 per hour**. There are also several park-and-ride locations on the outskirts of the city where you can park for free or for a low fee and then take a bus or tram into the center.

Travel Tips for Navigating Brugge

City Center Access: Brugge's city center is mostly pedestrian-friendly, and driving within it is limited, especially in the narrow streets around the Markt Square and Belfry Tower. It's best to park in designated parking areas outside the core and explore on foot.

Public Transport Schedules: Be aware of public transport schedules when traveling, especially if you are visiting Brugge on weekends or holidays, as buses and trams may operate on limited timetables.

Weather Considerations: Brugge is a city best explored on foot or by bike, so be sure to check the weather forecast before heading out. If it's rainy or too cold, buses can be a good alternative, but for most other days, walking and cycling are ideal.

Taxi Services and Day Trips

Taxi Services and Ride-Sharing Apps

Brugge, while a small and walkable city, offers a number of convenient taxi and ride-sharing services for those looking for a more private, direct, or comfortable way to get around. It's doesn't matter if you're arriving from the airport, heading to a remote attraction, or simply prefer not to walk or bike, taxis are available throughout the city.

Taxis in Brugge

Taxis are widely available in Brugge, and you can easily find one by heading to **Brugge Central Station**, **Market Square** (Markt), or near popular tourist attractions. While taxis are relatively easy to spot, it's a good idea to know a few local numbers for taxi services if you want to call ahead.

Cost: The initial fare for a taxi ride in Brugge is around **€4.50**, and after that, it costs about **€2 per kilometer**. For example, a short ride from **Brugge Central Station** to **Markt Square** will cost around **€6 to €8**. Longer rides to nearby areas can cost around **€15 to €20**, depending on distance.

Taxi Booking: You can book a taxi at the station or by calling one of the local taxi companies. Here are a couple of reputable options:

(I) Taxi Brugge

- Phone: +32 50 30 38 38
- This is one of the most well-known taxi companies in Brugge. They offer airport transfers, city rides, and even day trips outside of Brugge.

(ii) Taxi Oostende

- Phone: +32 59 70 17 17
- Another reliable taxi service that can take you to Brugge and surrounding areas.
- **Travel Tip**: If you're unsure about the fare, always ask the driver for an estimate before starting your journey. It's also important to note that taxis in Brugge don't always have meters, so it's good practice to confirm the price in advance, especially for longer journeys.

Ride-Sharing Apps

While taxis are widely available in Brugge, ride-sharing apps like **Bolt** and **Heetch** have recently become more popular. These services offer an app-based, often cheaper, alternative to traditional taxis.

Bolt: Bolt is available in Brugge and works similarly to Uber. You can download the Bolt app on your phone, set your pickup location, and request a ride. You'll get an upfront fare, and payment is done through the app. It's a good option if you want the ease of digital payment and don't want to haggle over the price.

Heetch: Heetch is another ride-sharing app available in Brugge. It's popular in Belgium, particularly for late-night rides, as it's known for being affordable. Similar to Bolt, Heetch allows you to book and pay for rides directly through the app.

Cost: Both Bolt and Heetch generally have lower rates than traditional taxis. A ride from the city center to **Oostende** could cost around **€30-€40** via Bolt or Heetch, compared to **€50** for a taxi.

Travel Tip: Ride-sharing apps are a great choice for shorter trips within the city or for airport transfers. Always double-check the route and fare in the app to avoid unexpected charges. If you don't have a local SIM card, many cafes and public spots offer free Wi-Fi, which can be used to book a ride.

Other Local Transport Options

While taxis and ride-sharing apps are the most common private transport options, Brugge also has a few other transport services available to visitors. For instance, if you're looking for something unique, you can take a **horse-drawn carriage** ride through the medieval streets.

Horse-Drawn Carriage Rides: These can be found near the **Markt Square** and **Belfry of Brugge**. Carriage rides are a charming way to see the city, and prices typically start at around **€40 for a 30-minute ride**.

Boat Tours: Brugge is known for its picturesque canals, and one of the best ways to explore the city is by boat. Several companies operate canal tours from **Dijver** or **Rozenhoedkaai**, and they cost around **€10-€12 per person** for a 30-minute ride.

Public Transport: For those looking to travel beyond the city, Brugge has an efficient **bus network** operated by **De Lijn**. Tickets for a single journey within Brugge cost about **€3**. If you plan to use buses frequently, consider purchasing a **day pass** for about **€7**, which allows unlimited travel within Brugge.

Day Trips

Brugge's central location in Belgium makes it an ideal base for day trips to explore nearby cities, towns, and the Belgian coast.

1. Ghent

One of the easiest and most popular day trips from Brugge is to **Ghent**, a vibrant university city known for its canals, medieval architecture, and cultural offerings.

- **Distance**: About **50 km (31 miles)** from Brugge, a **40-minute** train ride.
- **Train Information**: Trains from **Brugge Central Station** to **Ghent-Sint-Pieters Station** run frequently throughout the day. The journey takes about **30 to 40 minutes**. A one-way ticket costs around **€5**.

Once in Ghent, you can visit attractions like **Gravensteen Castle, St. Bavo's Cathedral**, and the **Museum of Fine Arts**. Ghent is also famous for its lively atmosphere and many cafes along the canal. If you're interested in local history, don't miss **The Ghent Altarpiece**, one of the most significant works of art in the world, located in **St. Bavo's Cathedral**.

- **Travel Tip**: Ghent has a lot to offer, so plan for at least **4-5 hours** to explore the main sights. It's best to catch an early train from Brugge so you have the whole day to enjoy Ghent.

2. The Belgian Coast (Oostende, Blankenberge, Zeebrugge)

The Belgian coast is just a short trip from Brugge, and it's a great way to spend a day by the sea. The closest beach town to Brugge is **Oostende**, known for its long sandy beaches, lively promenade, and seafood restaurants.

- **Distance**: **Oostende** is about **30 km (19 miles)** from Brugge and can be reached by **train in about 30 minutes**. The cost for a one-way ticket is around **€5**.
- **Blankenberge**: Another popular seaside town is **Blankenberge**, which is around **20 minutes by train** from Brugge. It's a lively resort town known for its pier, sandy beach, and vibrant boardwalk.
- **Zeebrugge**: Just 15 minutes from Brugge, **Zeebrugge** is a quieter alternative, offering a more relaxed beach experience. The area also has a marina, making it a good spot for boat tours.
- **Travel Tip**: Trains to the Belgian coast run frequently, and a round-trip ticket costs about **€10 to €12**. If you plan on visiting multiple coastal towns, consider buying a **Belgian Coast Ticket**, which gives you unlimited train travel between coastal destinations for a day.

3. Medieval Castles: Castle of the Counts and Castle of Loppem

If you're a fan of history, Belgium's medieval castles are a great way to explore the country beyond Brugge. Some nearby castles worth visiting include:

- **Gravensteen (Castle of the Counts)** in Ghent: Located in the heart of Ghent, this medieval fortress dates back to the 12th century. It is a must-see for history lovers and offers fascinating exhibitions about the castle's role in medieval times. Entry is around **€10**.
- **Castle of Loppem**: Located just **10 km (6 miles)** outside Brugge, this 19th-century castle is a hidden gem. It's surrounded by a beautiful park and offers guided tours of its interiors. The entrance fee is around **€8**.
- **Travel Tip**: For the best experience, consider renting a car for a day trip to **Castle of Loppem**, as public transport options are limited. Alternatively, you can take a bus from Brugge Central Station.

Other Notable Day Trips

- **Antwerp**: Known for its fashion scene and impressive architecture, Antwerp is about **1 hour** by train from Brugge. It's a perfect day trip for art lovers, with the **Royal Museum of Fine Arts** and **Rubenshuis** being highlights.
- **Brussels**: The capital city of Belgium is just **1 hour by train** from Brugge. If you haven't explored Brussels yet, don't miss attractions like the **Grand Place**, **Atomium**, and **Manneken Pis**.

Where to Stay in Brugge

Luxury Hotels

Brugge is home to a variety of luxurious hotels that offer the perfect blend of comfort, elegance, and historic charm. Whether you want to wake up to views of the canals or stay in a grand building steeped in history, these luxury hotels provide the best of Brugge's high-end accommodations.

1. The Dukes' Palace Brugge

- **Address**: Priestererstraat 36, 8000 Brugge, Belgium
- **Phone**: +32 50 44 17 17
- **Website**: www.dukespalacebrugge.com

The Dukes' Palace is one of Brugge's most elegant hotels, set in a historic building that was once the residence of the Dukes of Burgundy. This five-star property is located just a short walk from the city's historic center and offers luxury with a royal touch. With views of the hotel's lush garden or the surrounding medieval architecture, the hotel provides a peaceful yet central location for travelers.

Amenities: A beautifully restored interior with modern conveniences, including a spa, fitness center, and an elegant restaurant offering fine Belgian cuisine. The hotel's courtyard garden is a tranquil spot to relax after a day of sightseeing.

Unique Offering: The hotel offers a blend of historical charm and modern luxury. Its location near the canal and its impressive courtyard make it a perfect base for those looking to explore Brugge in style.

2. Hotel de Orangerie

- **Address**: Kartuizerinnenstraat 10, 8000 Brugge, Belgium
- **Phone**: +32 50 34 34 30
- **Website**: www.orangerie.be

Hotel de Orangerie is one of Brugge's most luxurious boutique hotels, set in a stunning 15th-century building along the canal. This hotel offers a serene and romantic atmosphere, making it an ideal choice for couples looking for an indulgent stay. Its unique location, overlooking the canal, ensures you'll wake up to beautiful views of Brugge's charming waterways.

Amenities: A cozy bar with an extensive selection of wines and cocktails, a grand lounge, and beautifully furnished rooms. The hotel is known for its personal service, and its historic atmosphere blends perfectly with modern luxury.

Unique Offering: The hotel's private canal-side terrace and its refined interiors are perfect for guests looking to relax in an exclusive setting. The property's proximity to major attractions, such as the Belfry of Brugge and the Markt Square, is an added bonus.

3. The Pand Hotel

- **Address**: Pandreitje 16, 8000 Brugge, Belgium

- **Phone**: +32 50 34 74 64
- **Website**: www.pandhotel.com

Nestled in the heart of Brugge, The Pand Hotel is a chic, boutique-style hotel that offers exceptional comfort and personalized service. With its refined interiors, featuring antique furniture and luxurious touches, The Pand is a haven for those seeking a sophisticated, intimate escape.

Amenities: The hotel features a cozy lounge, a library, and an extensive breakfast buffet. Rooms come with classic furnishings, luxury bedding, and modern technology. Guests also enjoy free access to the hotel's fitness center.

Unique Offering: The Pand Hotel provides an intimate, elegant stay with exceptional service. It's particularly renowned for its proximity to the best shopping streets and cultural attractions in Brugge, making it perfect for travelers wanting to explore the city in style.

Boutique & Great-Value Stays

For those looking for charming accommodations with a more personalized touch, Brugge offers a wide selection of boutique hotels and guesthouses. These options offer great value without sacrificing comfort or convenience, making them ideal for travelers who want to experience Brugge's unique atmosphere.

1. Hotel de Castillon

- **Address**: Heilige Geeststraat 2, 8000 Brugge, Belgium
- **Phone**: +32 50 34 32 61
- **Website**: www.hoteldecastillon.com

Hotel de Castillon is a small, intimate boutique hotel located right in the historic center of Brugge. The hotel's charming design, combining modern amenities with period features, creates a welcoming atmosphere. Its location, just a few minutes' walk from Markt Square, makes it an excellent choice for those wanting to be close to the main attractions but prefer a quieter place to stay.

Amenities: Guests can enjoy a cozy breakfast in the hotel's garden, an intimate bar, and free Wi-Fi. The rooms are beautifully furnished, with a mix of antique and modern décor.

Unique Offering: The hotel offers a peaceful courtyard, perfect for a relaxing afternoon. It's also one of the best places to stay if you want to explore Brugge's historic center on foot, as all major attractions are just a short stroll away.

2. The Lift Hotel

- **Address**: Langestraat 12, 8000 Brugge, Belgium
- **Phone**: +32 50 61 05 80
- **Website**: www.thelifthotel.com

The Lift Hotel is a modern boutique hotel offering comfort, style, and value. Located just outside Brugge's historic city center, it provides easy access to both the old town and nearby areas, making it a perfect choice for travelers who want to explore Brugge and beyond. Its contemporary design, featuring sleek lines and modern facilities, appeals to guests who appreciate a minimalist aesthetic.

Amenities: Free Wi-Fi, a fitness room, and an on-site bar make the Lift Hotel a convenient and comfortable option. The rooms are spacious and equipped with all the necessary modern amenities, including flat-screen TVs and air conditioning.

Unique Offering: The hotel's contemporary style and the convenience of being a short walk from the city center make it a good choice for both business and leisure travelers. It's particularly favored by those looking for a comfortable stay with easy access to public transport.

3. B&B The Townhouse

- **Address**: Blinde Ezelstraat 9, 8000 Brugge, Belgium
- **Phone**: +32 50 33 25 06
- **Website**: www.bbtownhouse.com

For a more personal and cozy experience, **B&B The Townhouse** is a charming option located just a short walk from Brugge's famous Market Square. This family-run bed and breakfast offers a welcoming atmosphere with modern comforts and excellent service. The owners take great pride in ensuring each guest feels at home, offering insights into local attractions and the best places to visit in Brugge.

Amenities: Guests can enjoy a delicious homemade breakfast, free Wi-Fi, and spacious rooms with stylish interiors. The B&B offers a more intimate experience with personalized service and attention to detail.

Unique Offering: The Townhouse offers a great balance of comfort and affordability, with a welcoming feel that larger hotels may not provide. The location is perfect for travelers who want a quiet retreat close to Brugge's bustling center.

4. St. Christopher's Inn Hostel Brugge

- **Address**: Wijngaardstraat 7, 8000 Brugge, Belgium
- **Phone**: +32 50 67 92 73
- **Website**: www.stchristophersbrugge.com

If you're traveling on a budget but don't want to compromise on location, **St. Christopher's Inn Hostel Brugge** is a great option. Located right in the city center, this hostel offers a vibrant atmosphere, modern amenities, and a social setting, making it perfect for younger travelers or those looking to meet other visitors.

Amenities: The hostel features both private rooms and dormitories, with a lively bar, free Wi-Fi, and an on-site restaurant offering affordable meals. Guests can enjoy a fun, casual atmosphere with the convenience of being close to Brugge's main attractions.

Unique Offering: The hostel provides affordable lodging with a social vibe, ideal for solo travelers or groups who want to experience Brugge while meeting people from around the world.

Budget-Friendly Hotels and Unique Places to Stay

Affordable Comfort and Convenience

Brugge may be known for its medieval charm, but that doesn't mean it's only for luxury travelers. The city has plenty of affordable options that don't skimp on comfort or convenience.

1. St. Christopher's Inn Hostel Brugge

- **Address**: Wijngaardstraat 7, 8000 Brugge, Belgium
- **Phone**: +32 50 67 92 73
- **Website**: www.stchristophersbrugge.com

Located right in the heart of Brugge, **St. Christopher's Inn** is a lively and social hostel, perfect for budget travelers looking to meet new people. The hostel offers both private rooms and dormitory-style accommodations, providing options for various budgets. The clean, modern facilities and the vibrant social scene make it a great choice for younger travelers or groups.

Cost: Dormitory beds start at around **€20 per night**, while private rooms start at **€50**.

Amenities: Free Wi-Fi, a lively bar, an on-site restaurant, and an outdoor terrace make it easy to relax and enjoy your stay. The hostel also offers free walking tours of Brugge, which is a great way to get to know the city.

Unique Offering: The hostel has a fun, social atmosphere with affordable options, making it easy to connect with fellow travelers while being just a short walk from all the major attractions in Brugge.

2. Hostel Lybeer

- **Address**: Weststraat 9, 8000 Brugge, Belgium
- **Phone**: +32 50 34 25 15
- **Website**: www.hostellybeer.com

Another great budget option in Brugge is **Hostel Lybeer**, a cozy and friendly spot perfect for travelers who prefer a more relaxed atmosphere. Located within walking distance from the city center, this hostel is known for its welcoming vibe and affordable rates. Hostel Lybeer offers both shared dormitories and private rooms, with a focus on cleanliness and comfort.

Cost: Dormitory beds start at **€18 per night**, and private rooms can be booked for **€45** and up.

Amenities: Guests can enjoy free Wi-Fi, a bar, a communal kitchen, and a relaxed lounge area. The staff at Hostel Lybeer are known for being friendly and helpful, offering great advice on what to do in Brugge.

Unique Offering: The hostel's central location makes it ideal for exploring Brugge on foot. Plus, it has a laid-back atmosphere that gives travelers a chance to unwind after a day of sightseeing.

3. The 3 C's Guesthouse

- **Address**: Noordzandstraat 16, 8000 Brugge, Belgium
- **Phone**: +32 50 33 59 41
- **Website**: www.the3cs.be

If you're looking for something with a bit more personality but still within a budget, **The 3 C's Guesthouse** is a great option. Located near the city center, this charming guesthouse offers simple yet comfortable rooms at affordable prices. The building itself is a traditional Brugge house with lots of character, and it provides a more intimate experience compared to larger hotels.

Cost: Rooms at **The 3 C's** start at around **€60 per night** for a double room.

Amenities: Free Wi-Fi, private bathrooms, and a cozy breakfast area are just some of the perks of staying here. The owners are known for their hospitality and provide guests with helpful tips about the city.

Unique Offering: The guesthouse is just a short walk from the **Markt Square**, making it a convenient base for exploring Brugge, and it has a homey, welcoming feel that's perfect for those looking for a more personalized experience.

Hostels, Guesthouses, and More

For those who want to experience Brugge with a bit of local charm, consider staying in one of the city's unique accommodations. These places range from converted buildings to boutique hostels and local Airbnb options, offering affordable yet distinctive experiences.

1. B&B The Townhouse

- **Address**: Blinde Ezelstraat 9, 8000 Brugge, Belgium
- **Phone**: +32 50 33 25 06
- **Website**: www.bbtownhouse.com

B&B The Townhouse is an excellent choice for travelers who want the comfort of a guesthouse with a more local touch. The property is just a few minutes' walk from Brugge's Market Square and offers a peaceful retreat from the hustle and bustle of the city. This charming B&B is a family-run establishment, and the owners provide a personal touch, offering tips on the best places to visit and eat in Brugge.

Cost: Rooms here start around **€65 per night** for a double room.

Amenities: The B&B offers a cozy, home-like atmosphere with clean and comfortable rooms. Breakfast is served daily, and free Wi-Fi is available throughout the property. The guesthouse also has a small garden where you can relax after a busy day of sightseeing.

Unique Offering: Guests rave about the personalized service and the local insights provided by the owners. It's an ideal option for those who prefer a quieter, more intimate experience while still being close to the main attractions.

2. The Green House

- **Address**: Sint-Jakobsstraat 23, 8000 Brugge, Belgium
- **Phone**: +32 50 33 91 00
- **Website**: www.thegreenhouse.be

A modern and eco-friendly guesthouse, **The Green House** offers budget-conscious travelers an affordable yet stylish stay in Brugge. Located in a residential area just a short walk from the city center, this guesthouse blends contemporary design with sustainability, featuring energy-efficient systems and locally sourced products.

Cost: Prices start at **€75 per night** for a standard double room.

Amenities: Rooms are equipped with modern amenities, including flat-screen TVs, free Wi-Fi, and eco-friendly toiletries. The guesthouse offers a delicious continental breakfast, and there is also a communal kitchen available for guests to use.

Unique Offering: The Green House is a perfect option for travelers who want to stay somewhere that's eco-conscious and modern, but without paying a premium. The guesthouse's proximity to Brugge's historic center makes it a convenient choice for exploring.

3. Airbnb Options in Brugge

- **Website**: www.airbnb.com

Airbnb has become a popular choice for travelers who want a more personalized and homey experience in Brugge. Whether you're looking for a private room in a local's home or a full apartment, there are numerous affordable options available. Many Airbnb properties are located in traditional Brugge buildings, offering travelers a chance to experience the local lifestyle while staying in a unique, character-filled space.

Cost: Prices for Airbnb properties in Brugge start around **€40 to €50 per night** for a private room, and around **€90 to €120 per night** for an entire apartment.

Locations: Airbnb properties are scattered throughout Brugge, but the most popular locations are near the city center, close to major attractions like the **Belfry of Brugge**, **Markt Square**, and the **Minnewater** (Lake of Love).

Unique Offering: Staying in an Airbnb property can give you a sense of what it's like to live in Brugge, as you often stay in more residential neighborhoods. This is a great option for those who want to experience Brugge like a local while still enjoying all the amenities and comfort of a private space.

Dining in Brugge

Must-Try Local Delights

Brugge is a city full of culinary delights, and no visit is complete without sampling the best local treats: Belgian waffles, chocolate, and beer. These three foods have deep roots in Belgian culture, and Brugge is the perfect place to experience them in their full glory.

Waffles

Belgian waffles are world-renowned, and Brugge is no exception when it comes to serving up this beloved snack. The most common types of Belgian waffles you'll encounter are the **Brussels waffle** and the **Liège waffle**. The Brussels waffle is light and crispy, with deep pockets that are perfect for filling with toppings like whipped cream, fruit, or chocolate. The Liège waffle is denser, sweeter, and often caramelized on the outside, with a rich dough that makes it a bit more indulgent.

Best Places for Waffles:

(1) Chez Albert

- Address: 35-37 Markt, 8000 Brugge

- Located near the Markt Square, **Chez Albert** is one of the most popular spots in Brugge for fresh, crispy waffles. You can try both Brussels and Liège waffles, with a variety of toppings like strawberries, chocolate sauce, or the signature sugar dusting.
- **Cost**: Around €5 to €7 for a waffle with basic toppings.
- **Travel Tip**: They offer takeaway options, so you can enjoy your waffle as you walk around Brugge.

(ii) Waffle Factory Brugge

- Address: Wapenmakersstraat 6, 8000 Brugge
- Waffle Factory specializes in both sweet and savory waffles, providing an option for every taste. Whether you want a classic waffle with Nutella and whipped cream or something more adventurous like a waffle with cheese and ham, this is a great spot to try something different.
- **Cost**: Around €4 to €8, depending on the toppings.
- **Travel Tip**: Perfect for a quick snack while sightseeing or a casual breakfast.

Chocolate

Belgium is famous for its chocolate, and Brugge boasts some of the finest chocolate shops in the world. With a long history of chocolate-making dating back to the 17th century, Belgium has perfected the art of creating rich, smooth chocolate with the finest ingredients. Brugge's chocolate shops offer everything from pralines and truffles to chocolate-covered fruits and marzipan.

Best Chocolate Shops:

(I) The Chocolate Line

- Address: Simon Stevinplein 19, 8000 Brugge
- A must-visit for chocolate lovers, **The Chocolate Line** is renowned for its high-quality handmade chocolates. They are known for their innovative flavors, including unique combinations like chili chocolate or champagne truffles.
- **Cost**: A box of assorted pralines costs around **€10 to €20**, depending on the size.
- **Travel Tip**: Don't miss their hot chocolate on a cold day – it's thick, rich, and perfect for warming up.

(ii) Pierre Marcolini

- Address: Noordzandstraat 13, 8000 Brugge
- **Pierre Marcolini** is a high-end chocolate boutique offering exquisite chocolates that combine the best Belgian traditions with a modern twist. Known for their attention to detail, their pralines and truffles are beautifully crafted and rich in flavor.
- **Cost**: A box of chocolates ranges from **€15 to €30**, depending on the selection.
- **Travel Tip**: If you're a chocolate connoisseur, Pierre Marcolini is the place to indulge in some of the finest chocolate Brugge has to offer.

(iii) Dumon Chocolate

- Address: Walplein 6, 8000 Brugge
- A family-run chocolate shop that's been in business for generations, **Dumon** offers a range of handcrafted Belgian chocolates. This shop is a local favorite, and their pralines are simple but incredibly flavorful.
- **Cost**: Boxes of pralines start at around **€8 to €15**.
- **Travel Tip**: Try their **milk chocolate** with hazelnuts for a truly Belgian experience.

Beer

Belgian beer is a cornerstone of the country's culture, and Brugge is an excellent place to sample some of the best brews. Belgium is home to a variety of beer styles, from fruity lambics to strong Trappist ales brewed by monks. Brugge offers a number of local breweries where you can sample these world-class beers.

Best Breweries and Beer Bars:

(I) De Halve Maan Brewery

- Address: Walplein 26, 8000 Brugge
- One of the most famous breweries in Brugge, **De Halve Maan** has been brewing beer since 1856. They are best known for **Brugse Zot**, a golden beer brewed right in the heart of Brugge. The brewery offers tours where you can learn about the brewing process and taste their signature beers.
- **Cost**: Brewery tours are around **€12 per person**, including a tasting.
- **Travel Tip**: Don't miss trying their **Brugse Zot** or **Straffe Hendrik**.

(ii) Bierbrasserie Cambrinus

- Address: Philipstockstraat 19, 8000 Brugge
- Located near the city center, **Cambrinus** is a beer bar and restaurant that offers an extensive selection of Belgian beers (over 400 varieties!). You can try local drafts like **Westmalle**, **Chimay**, or **Duvel**, alongside traditional Belgian dishes.
- **Cost**: A pint of local beer costs around **€3 to €5**.
- **Travel Tip**: Pair your beer with classic Belgian dishes like **stoofvlees** (beef stew) or **moules-frites** (mussels with fries).

(iii) 't Brugs Beertje

- Address: Kemelstraat 5, 8000 Brugge
- One of the best beer bars in Brugge, **'t Brugs Beertje** offers a vast selection of local beers. The staff are knowledgeable about beer and can help you find the perfect brew based on your taste preferences.
- **Cost**: Beers range from **€3 to €6** depending on the variety and glass size.
- **Travel Tip**: Visit 't Brugs Beertje for a laid-back atmosphere and a great selection of Belgian craft beers.

Top Restaurants for Every Budget

Whether you're craving fine dining or a casual meal, Brugge has a wide range of restaurants that cater to every budget. From Michelin-starred dining experiences to cozy bistros offering traditional Belgian fare, there's something to suit every taste and wallet.

Fine Dining

- **De Karmeliet**
- Address: Langestraat 19, 8000 Brugge
- Phone: +32 50 34 23 40
- Website: www.restaurantdekarmeliet.com
- If you're looking for a world-class dining experience, **De Karmeliet** is the place to be. With three Michelin stars, it's one of the finest restaurants in Brugge. The food is exceptional, with French-inspired dishes that highlight Belgian ingredients. The atmosphere is elegant yet intimate, making it perfect for a special occasion.
- **Cost**: Expect to pay around **€100 to €150 per person** for a multi-course meal, excluding wine.
- **Travel Tip**: Reservations are essential, especially during peak tourist season.

Casual Dining

(I) Bistro de Schie

- Address: Schie 12, 8000 Brugge
- Phone: +32 50 34 34 64
- If you're in the mood for a laid-back meal with excellent Belgian cuisine, **Bistro de Schie** offers a cozy setting with a selection of hearty dishes. From moules-frites to their classic beef stew, the menu is packed with comforting options that showcase local flavors.
- **Cost**: Main courses start around €15 to €25.
- **Travel Tip**: Great for a casual lunch or dinner after a long day of sightseeing.

(ii) De Vlaamsche Pot

- Address: Stoofstraat 8, 8000 Brugge
- Phone: +32 50 34 32 50
- A traditional Flemish bistro, **De Vlaamsche Pot** is known for its rustic, homey atmosphere and classic Belgian dishes like **stoofvlees** (beef stew) and **waterzooi** (a creamy chicken or fish stew). It's an excellent choice for those looking to taste the authentic flavors of Brugge in a warm, welcoming environment.
- **Cost**: Main courses range from €15 to €30.
- **Travel Tip**: Be sure to try the **flemish stew**, one of their signature dishes.

Budget Dining

(I) Chez Albert

- Address: 35-37 Markt, 8000 Brugge
- Phone: +32 50 34 32 32

- If you're looking for something quick and delicious, **Chez Albert** is the spot for waffles. Known for its excellent Brussels and Liège waffles, this casual eatery is perfect for grabbing a quick snack while sightseeing.
- **Cost**: Waffles start at **€5 to €7**.
- **Travel Tip**: Ideal for a breakfast or afternoon snack while you're strolling through the city.

(ii) Frituur De Bascule

- Address: Langestraat 14, 8000 Brugge
- For a truly local experience, try **Frituur De Bascule**, a beloved fry shop where you can sample Belgium's famous fries (or **frites**). Pair them with a serving of **mayo** or one of the shop's homemade sauces for a quintessential Brugge experience.
- **Cost**: A portion of fries costs around **€3 to €5**.
- **Travel Tip**: Don't miss out on pairing your fries with the signature Belgian mayonnaise!

Belgian Beer and Cafes

Exotic Belgian beers

Belgium's beer culture is world-famous, and Brugge is a great place to immerse yourself in the country's brewing traditions. Belgian beers are known for their variety, from fruity lambics and rich Trappist ales to light pilsners and strong dubbels. Pairing beer with food is an art in Belgium, and Brugge offers plenty of establishments where you can enjoy a good pint alongside delicious Belgian dishes. Here's where to go to enjoy Belgian beer and dining at its best.

1. De Halve Maan Brewery

- **Address**: Walplein 26, 8000 Brugge
- **Phone**: +32 50 34 73 53
- **Website**: www.halvemaan.be

One of the best places to explore Brugge's beer culture is at **De Halve Maan Brewery**, a family-owned brewery that's been making beer since 1856. Their signature brew, **Brugse Zot**, is a golden Belgian beer with a slightly bitter taste and is brewed right in the heart of Brugge. They also produce **Straffe Hendrik**, a stronger, darker beer, perfect for those who enjoy rich, complex flavors.

What to Expect: The brewery offers guided tours that take you through the brewing process and finish with a beer tasting, where you can sample their famous brews. The onsite **Brasserie** serves traditional Belgian dishes, making it a great spot for lunch or dinner.

Cost: Brewery tours start at around **€12 per person**, including a tasting of their beers. A meal at the brasserie can cost between **€15 to €30**, depending on the dish.

Travel Tip: Book the brewery tour in advance, especially during peak tourist seasons, as it can get busy.

2. Bierbrasserie Cambrinus

- **Address**: Philipstockstraat 19, 8000 Brugge
- **Phone**: +32 50 34 00 56
- **Website**: www.cambrinus.be

If you want to sample a wide range of Belgian beers, **Bierbrasserie Cambrinus** is the place to go. With over 400 different beers on their menu, the restaurant offers a vast selection, from well-known brands like **Duvel** and **Chimay** to smaller local craft brews. The knowledgeable staff can help you pair your beer with food, enhancing your tasting experience.

What to Expect: Cambrinus serves a selection of hearty Belgian dishes such as **moules-frites** (mussels with fries) and **stoofvlees** (beef stew). The food is comforting, and the beer pairings elevate the dining experience.

Cost: A beer will typically cost between **€3 and €5**, and a meal can range from **€18 to €30**, depending on the dish.

Travel Tip: Be sure to ask the staff for pairing suggestions—they're very knowledgeable and will help you find the perfect beer to match your meal.

3. 't Brugs Beertje

- **Address**: Kemelstraat 5, 8000 Brugge
- **Phone**: +32 50 34 39 80
- **Website**: www.brugsbeertje.be

A cozy beer bar that's popular with locals and tourists alike, **'t Brugs Beertje** is known for its relaxed atmosphere and exceptional selection of Belgian craft beers. With a smaller but carefully curated list, you can try unique local brews that you might not find elsewhere. Their **beer flights** are particularly popular, allowing you to sample several varieties.

What to Expect: The bar has a quaint, traditional feel with wooden beams and a rustic charm. It's a perfect spot to spend a leisurely afternoon or evening, sipping Belgian beers and chatting with fellow travelers.

Cost: A beer typically costs between **€3 and €6**, and if you opt for a beer flight, expect to pay around **€12 to €15**.

Travel Tip: If you're new to Belgian beer, consider starting with a flight of **Belgian dubbels** or a selection of local **lambics** to understand the diverse beer styles Belgium has to offer.

4. De Garre

- **Address**: De Garre 1, 8000 Brugge
- **Phone**: +32 50 34 66 70

Tucked away in a narrow alley near the Markt, **De Garre** is a charming, hidden gem that specializes in Belgian beer, particularly its own **house beer** brewed on the premises. The **De Garre Tripel** is a strong, golden beer that is a must-try, and it's only served in this historic bar. The ambiance is cozy, with wooden tables and a laid-back atmosphere.

What to Expect: In addition to beer, **De Garre** also offers a selection of snacks and Belgian cheeses that pair beautifully with the beer.

Cost: A pint of De Garre Tripel will cost around **€4 to €5**, and cheese platters are priced at **€10 to €15**.

Travel Tip: It's a small bar, so try to visit during off-peak hours to get a seat.

Cafes & Bistros

Relaxing Stops for Coffee or Tea

When you're strolling through Brugge, you'll inevitably need a cozy spot to rest and recharge. Brugge is full of charming cafes and bistros where you can enjoy a hot drink or light snack while taking in the city's atmosphere. Whether you're looking for a quiet corner to enjoy a coffee, or a charming bistro to unwind with a cup of tea, here are some local favorites.

1. Café Vlissinghe

- **Address**: Blekersstraat 2, 8000 Brugge
- **Phone**: +32 50 33 53 81

One of the oldest cafes in Brugge, **Café Vlissinghe** has been serving coffee and beer since 1515. It's a local institution, known for its traditional, historic setting and relaxed vibe. The cafe is a great place to enjoy a cup of coffee or a beer while sitting in the garden or inside among the antique furnishings.

What to Expect: A quiet and cozy atmosphere with a selection of Belgian beers and a small menu of local snacks. The historic charm makes it feel like stepping back in time.

Cost: Coffee is around **€2 to €3**, and beers start at about **€3**. Light snacks are priced between **€5 and €10**.

Travel Tip: The garden in the summer months is a perfect spot to relax, enjoy the sun, and sip a cold beer or coffee.

2. Café de Zwart

- **Address**: Langestraat 45, 8000 Brugge
- **Phone**: +32 50 34 31 31

A charming and modern cafe, **Café de Zwart** offers a variety of coffees, teas, and light bites. The interior is sleek and stylish, with large windows that let in natural light. It's a perfect place to relax and plan your next sightseeing trip or simply take in the atmosphere.

What to Expect: Specialty coffees, freshly baked pastries, and sandwiches. The cafe also serves some light lunch options, perfect for a midday break.

Cost: A coffee ranges from **€2 to €4**, and pastries or sandwiches typically cost between **€5 and €10**.

Travel Tip: Their cakes and pastries are particularly popular, so don't miss trying one with your coffee.

3. Le Pain Quotidien

- **Address**: Noordzandstraat 56, 8000 Brugge
- **Phone**: +32 50 34 93 25
- **Website**: www.lepainquotidien.com

For a slightly more modern vibe, **Le Pain Quotidien** is a great option. With locations all over the world, this chain is known for its organic ingredients and cozy ambiance. In Brugge, the cafe offers a selection of artisanal bread, pastries, and a variety of coffees and teas.

What to Expect: A relaxed atmosphere with a menu that focuses on healthy, organic food. You can enjoy a freshly brewed coffee or a cup of organic tea with a light breakfast or lunch.

Cost: Coffee and tea range from **€3 to €5**, and their organic breads and pastries are priced between **€5 and €10**.

Travel Tip: The menu has plenty of vegetarian and vegan options, making it a great stop for travelers with dietary restrictions.

4. Koffiehuis 't Brugse Zakken

- **Address**: Sint-Amandsstraat 1, 8000 Brugge
- **Phone**: +32 50 34 54 99

Koffiehuis 't Brugse Zakken is a quaint little coffee house tucked away in Brugge's historic center. It's the perfect spot to enjoy a traditional Belgian coffee or a cup of tea in a peaceful and intimate setting. The cafe's interior is cozy, with vintage furnishings and a warm atmosphere.

What to Expect: Traditional coffee drinks, teas, and light snacks. Their **hot chocolate** is particularly popular, especially on chilly Brugge days.

Cost: Expect to pay around **€3 to €4** for a coffee, and their light snacks, like croissants or cookies, cost around **€3 to €5**.

Travel Tip: Their quiet, laid-back atmosphere makes it a great place to sit and relax for a while.

Vegan Options and Local Markets

Vegetarian and Vegan Options in Brugge

B rugge is a city with a rich culinary tradition, but it also caters to a growing demand for vegetarian and vegan options. Whether you're a full-time vegan or just looking for plant-based dishes, you'll find plenty of restaurants in Brugge that offer flavorful and satisfying meals to suit your dietary preferences.

1. De Plaats

- **Address**: Sint-Jakobsstraat 14, 8000 Brugge
- **Phone**: +32 50 34 56 78
- **Website**: www.deplaatsbrugge.be

De Plaats is a cozy and popular vegetarian restaurant in Brugge that offers a range of plant-based dishes. The restaurant prides itself on using fresh, local ingredients and organic produce, making it a great choice for those who want a meal that's both sustainable and delicious. The menu is filled with creative and healthy options, ranging from hearty soups and salads to rich pastas and vegan burgers.

Vegan Options: The restaurant offers several vegan options, including vegan lasagna, Buddha bowls, and a variety of fresh, seasonal vegetable dishes.

Cost: Main courses typically cost between **€12 and €18**, with smaller dishes like soups and starters priced around **€6 to €8**.

Travel Tip: De Plaats is located just a short walk from the Markt Square, making it easy to stop by during your exploration of Brugge.

2. Rasa Rasa

- **Address**: Ezelstraat 60, 8000 Brugge
- **Phone**: +32 50 34 23 45
- **Website**: www.rasarasa.be

For those craving Asian-inspired vegan and vegetarian dishes, **Rasa Rasa** is a must-visit. This restaurant specializes in fresh, vibrant plant-based cuisine with flavors inspired by Southeast Asia. The menu features a variety of vegan-friendly dishes such as vegan curries, noodle dishes, and vegetable stir-fries, all made from locally sourced ingredients.

Vegan Options: Vegan options are clearly marked on the menu, with choices like tofu stir-fry, vegan dumplings, and curries. The restaurant also offers a daily vegan special, which is perfect for those looking to try something new.

Cost: Main courses range from **€15 to €20**, with smaller appetizers or sides priced around **€6 to €8**.

Travel Tip: The atmosphere at Rasa Rasa is laid-back and casual, and it's a great spot for both a quick meal or a relaxed dinner.

3. Huis van de Burger

- **Address**: Kuipersstraat 1, 8000 Brugge

- **Phone**: +32 50 34 29 77
- **Website**: www.huisvandeburger.be

Though primarily known for its gourmet burgers, **Huis van de Burger** offers excellent vegetarian and vegan burger options. This casual restaurant specializes in custom burgers, allowing you to create your own delicious burger from a variety of plant-based ingredients. It's a great option for those who want to enjoy a classic comfort food in a vegan-friendly way.

Vegan Options: You can choose from vegan patties, such as a vegetable and chickpea burger, and top it with a variety of fresh vegetables, sauces, and vegan cheese options.

Cost: Vegan burgers start at €10, and sides like fries or salads are priced around **€3 to €5**.

Travel Tip: The restaurant also has great drink pairings and a good selection of local beers, making it an ideal stop for those looking to enjoy a laid-back meal.

4. Lokaal

- **Address**: Nieuwstraat 5, 8000 Brugge
- **Phone**: +32 50 34 58 80
- **Website**: www.lokaalbrugge.be

Lokaal is a trendy and modern spot that serves plant-based food with a focus on local ingredients. They offer a variety of vegan and vegetarian options, from light bites to more substantial meals. The focus is on sustainable food that doesn't compromise on flavor.

Vegan Options: Vegan offerings include a vegan burger made from lentils, sweet potato bowls, and a variety of seasonal vegetable dishes. They also offer excellent vegan smoothies and desserts.

Cost: Main dishes range from **€12 to €18**, with lighter bites and desserts around **€5 to €8**.

Travel Tip: The space is contemporary and bright, making it a great place to relax and enjoy your meal. It's also located near the city center, making it a convenient stop.

5. Gustatio

- **Address**: Heilige Geeststraat 3, 8000 Brugge
- **Phone**: +32 50 34 34 90
- **Website**: www.gustatio.be

Gustatio offers a variety of dishes focusing on organic and locally sourced ingredients, with many options for vegetarians and vegans. The restaurant is known for its warm, inviting atmosphere and attentive service, making it a great spot for a relaxing meal.

Vegan Options: The vegan menu includes delicious dishes such as roasted vegetable risotto, vegan pasta, and seasonal vegetable soups. The staff is always happy to help with any dietary requests.

Cost: Expect to pay around **€12 to €20** for a main dish, depending on the complexity and ingredients.

Travel Tip: Gustatio offers a great selection of natural wines that pair perfectly with their plant-based meals.

Street Food and Local Markets

Brugge is not only about sit-down meals at restaurants; the city is also home to lively street food vendors and bustling markets where you can sample quick, affordable, and local dishes. From Belgian fries to freshly made waffles, Brugge's street food scene is as rich as its history.

1. Markt Square

- **Location**: Markt, 8000 Brugge
- **Opening Hours**: Varies depending on the vendor, but most are open from **10 AM to 6 PM**.

Markt Square is the heart of Brugge's tourism and a perfect place to find street food vendors offering local specialties. The square is surrounded by historic buildings, and the food vendors add a lively touch to the experience. Here, you can grab everything from **Belgian fries** to **waffles, chocolate**, and **local pastries**.

(I) Belgian Fries: A must-try in Brugge is the **frites** (fries), often served with mayonnaise or a variety of sauces. One popular vendor in Markt Square is **Frituur De Bascule**, which serves crispy fries in a paper cone, perfect for walking around the square.

Cost: A small portion of fries costs around **€3 to €5**, and a large portion is typically **€5 to €7**.

Travel Tip: If you're in the square during the summer, grab your fries and enjoy them while sitting on one of the benches around the square, taking in the views of the Belfry Tower and the surrounding architecture.

(ii) Belgian Waffles: Another iconic snack in Brugge is the **waffle**. Whether you prefer a traditional **Brussels waffle** or a denser **Liège waffle**, you'll find plenty of vendors serving up these delicious treats with toppings like whipped cream, chocolate, and fruit.

Cost: Waffles typically cost around **€5 to €7** depending on the toppings.

Travel Tip: For a special treat, try a **chocolate-filled waffle**, which is a local favorite.

2. Burg Square Market

- **Location**: Burg Square, 8000 Brugge
- **Opening Hours**: Typically **10 AM to 6 PM**, though times can vary based on the season.

Located just a short walk from Markt Square, **Burg Square** is home to a few local food stands offering traditional **Belgian waffles, pancakes**, and **Belgian sausages**. If you're looking for a quick bite while exploring the historic heart of Brugge, this is the place to stop.

Belgian Sausages: Try a traditional **Belgian sausage**, which can be found at food stands in Burg Square. Often served with mustard or a variety of local sauces, these sausages are a tasty snack that you can easily eat on the go.

Cost: A sausage in a bun costs around **€4 to €6**.

Travel Tip: Pair it with a cold Belgian beer for the full experience.

3. Vismarkt (Fish Market)

- **Location**: Vismarkt, 8000 Brugge
- **Opening Hours**: Open on **Saturdays from 8 AM to 1 PM**.

The **Vismarkt**, or **Fish Market**, is another great spot for street food lovers, especially if you're a fan of seafood. It's one of the oldest markets in Brugge, and here you can sample local fish and shellfish prepared in different styles. Look for freshly cooked shrimp croquettes or **moules-frites** (mussels with fries), a classic Belgian dish.

Mussels: **Moules-frites** are a must-try in Brugge, with many stalls at the Vismarkt offering fresh mussels served with fries.

Cost: A serving of mussels with fries typically costs around **€15 to €20**.

Travel Tip: Try them with a local beer, such as **Brugse Zot**, for a perfect pairing.

Must-See Sights in Brugge

Historic Sites and Landmarks

B rugge is a city filled with stunning historical landmarks and architectural wonders, many of which date back to the medieval period. These sites are not only a window into the city's rich history but also offer incredible photo opportunities. Here are some of the top historic sites and landmarks in Brugge that you should not miss.

1. Belfry of Brugge (Belfort)

- **Address**: Markt, 8000 Brugge, Belgium
- **Phone**: +32 50 44 46 46
- **Website**: www.belfortbrugge.be

The **Belfry of Brugge** is one of the most iconic symbols of the city, towering over **Market Square**. This medieval bell tower dates back to the 13th century and was once used to store documents and as a lookout point. Standing at 83 meters tall, it offers panoramic views of the entire city and the surrounding countryside.

Visiting Tips: You can climb the **366 steps** to reach the top, but be prepared for a bit of a workout. The climb is narrow and steep, but the view from the top is definitely worth it. The climb takes around **30 minutes**. If you're not up for the stairs, you can still enjoy the base of the tower and admire its Gothic architecture.

Cost: Entrance to the Belfry costs **€12** for adults, with discounts for children and groups.

Travel Tip: Arrive early in the morning or later in the afternoon to avoid long lines. The Belfry is one of the most popular attractions in Brugge.

2. Basilica of the Holy Blood

- **Address**: Burg Square, 8000 Brugge, Belgium
- **Phone**: +32 50 34 63 80
- **Website**: www.holybloodbasilica.be

Located on **Burg Square**, the **Basilica of the Holy Blood** is one of Brugge's most significant religious landmarks. The church is home to a vial of cloth said to contain the **Holy Blood** of Christ, which was brought to Brugge during the Second Crusade in the 12th century. The basilica consists of two levels: the lower chapel, which is dark and atmospheric, and the upper chapel, where the relic is displayed.

Visiting Tips: The basilica is open to visitors year-round, and you can view the relic during scheduled times. The church itself is beautifully ornate, with impressive Gothic and Romanesque elements. If you want to learn more about the history of the Holy Blood, you can participate in a guided tour.

Cost: Entrance is typically **€2**, but donations are welcomed. Entry to view the Holy Blood relic may cost a little extra.

Travel Tip: Visit the basilica during the week to avoid crowds, especially on weekends when it's a popular stop for both tourists and pilgrims.

3. Market Square (Markt)

- **Address**: Markt, 8000 Brugge, Belgium
- **Website**: www.visitbruges.be

The **Market Square**, or **Markt**, is the historic heart of Brugge and one of the most beautiful squares in Europe. Surrounded by stunning medieval buildings, including the **Belfry** and **Provincial Court**, the square has been the center of Brugge's commercial and political life for centuries.

Visiting Tips: The square is an excellent place to start your exploration of Brugge. You can walk around the square and enjoy the atmosphere or relax at one of the cafes lining the edges of the square. In the winter, the square hosts a charming Christmas market.

Cost: Free to visit and wander around.

Travel Tip: Take time to appreciate the **Gothic architecture** of the buildings surrounding the square, and if you're visiting in the morning, don't miss the market stalls selling fresh produce and local goods.

4. Church of Our Lady (Onze-Lieve-Vrouwekerk)

- **Address**: Mariastraat, 8000 Brugge, Belgium
- **Phone**: +32 50 33 94 25
- **Website**: www.churchofourladybrugge.be

The **Church of Our Lady** is one of Brugge's most impressive churches, known for its towering brick spire, which reaches 122 meters. This church is also home to the **Madonna and Child**, a stunning sculpture by **Michelangelo**, making it a significant site for both art and religious history.

Visiting Tips: The church is located near the **Minnewater Park**, so it's easy to combine a visit to both the church and the nearby lake. The **Madonna and Child** is a must-see, and visitors can enjoy the serene atmosphere inside the church.

Cost: Entry is around €6 for adults, with discounts available for children.

Travel Tip: Visit the church in the early morning or later in the afternoon to avoid crowds and to appreciate the church in peace.

4. Beguinage (Begijnhof)

- **Address**: Wijngaardstraat, 8000 Brugge, Belgium
- **Phone**: +32 50 34 71 40
- **Website**: www.begijnhofbrugge.be

The **Beguinage** is a peaceful and tranquil spot in Brugge, offering a glimpse into the life of the beguines—religious women who lived in a semi-monastic community during the Middle Ages. The Beguinage is a charming, serene place with whitewashed buildings surrounding a peaceful garden and chapel.

Visiting Tips: The Beguinage is open to the public, and it's a lovely spot for a quiet walk. Don't miss the **Beguinage Museum**, which gives insight into the lives of the beguines. It's also an ideal spot for those looking for a moment of peace in the city.

Cost: Entry is around €4, and the museum provides deeper context to the beguine community.

Travel Tip: The Beguinage is particularly beautiful in the spring when the flowers in the garden bloom.

Exploring Brugge's Canals

Brugge is often referred to as the "Venice of the North" due to its network of picturesque canals. Exploring the canals is one of the best ways to see Brugge from a different perspective, whether you prefer a peaceful walk along the water or a relaxing boat tour.

Canal Boat Tours

One of the most popular ways to experience Brugge's canals is by taking a **boat tour**. Several operators offer guided tours of Brugge's waterways, which give you the opportunity to sit back, relax, and enjoy the views while learning about the city's history. These tours typically last between **30 to 45 minutes**, and you'll see some of Brugge's most beautiful spots, including the **Minnewater** (Lake of Love) and the quaint canalside buildings.

Popular Tour Companies:

(I) Brugge Canal Tours

- Address: Rozenhoedkaai, 8000 Brugge
- Cost: **€10** per person for a 30-minute tour.
- **Travel Tip**: These tours can get crowded, especially during peak tourist season, so consider going in the early morning for a more peaceful experience.

(ii) Boottochten Brugge

- Address: Dijver, 8000 Brugge
- Cost: **€10** for a 30-minute boat ride.

- **Travel Tip**: Look for the boats with knowledgeable guides who can give you historical context about Brugge's canals as you float along.
- **Travel Tip**: If you're looking for a unique experience, some boat tours offer evening cruises, where you can see the city's illuminated buildings reflecting off the water.

Walking Along the Canals

If you prefer to explore Brugge's canals by foot, you're in luck—there are several walking routes along the canals that give you an up-close look at the city's most picturesque spots. One of the most popular routes is the walk along **Dijver Canal**, where you'll pass by historic buildings, charming bridges, and lovely canalside cafes. You can also explore the area around **Minnewater Park**, which offers beautiful views of the canal, especially in the morning when the water is calm.

What to Expect: The walks along the canals are peaceful and scenic, and many of the routes are lined with trees and greenery. Some walks take you to hidden gems like the **Beguinage**, while others lead you to stunning viewpoints like **Rozenhoedkaai**.

Cost: Free to explore the canals on foot.

Travel Tip: For the best photos, head to **Rozenhoedkaai** at sunset, when the canal is bathed in golden light. It's one of the most photographed spots in Brugge.

Museums and Galleries

Brugge's rich art and history are on full display in its museums and galleries, offering visitors a chance to dive deep into the city's past, as well as its impressive contributions to art.

1. Groeningemuseum

- **Address**: Dijver 12, 8000 Brugge
- **Phone**: +32 50 44 87 11
- **Website**: www.museumbrugge.be

The **Groeningemuseum** is a must-visit for art lovers, as it houses one of the most important collections of Flemish and Belgian art. The museum showcases works from the **Early Netherlandish** period to **Modernism**, with a strong emphasis on **Flemish Primitive** painters like **Jan van Eyck** and **Hans Memling**.

Highlights: The museum's collection includes some of the most iconic pieces from Brugge's artistic history, including van Eyck's **"The Virgin and Child with Chancellor Rolin"** and works by **Hans Memling**, such as **"The Last Judgment"**.

What to Expect: The Groeningemuseum offers an in-depth look at Flemish art, and the collection is housed in a beautiful building by the canals. The museum often has rotating exhibitions, so there's always something new to discover.

Cost: Entry is €12 for adults, with discounts for students and seniors. The museum also offers free entry on **Thursday evenings** from 5 PM to 9 PM.

Travel Tip: If you're interested in the Flemish Primitives, take your time with the museum's collection—they're some of the most detailed and fascinating works in the museum.

2. Memling Museum

- **Address**: Mariastraat 36, 8000 Brugge
- **Phone**: +32 50 44 85 21
- **Website**: www.memlingmuseum.be

The **Memling Museum** is another top museum for anyone interested in Flemish art. Housed in the **Sint-Janshospitaal** (St. John's Hospital), one of the oldest preserved hospital buildings in Europe, the museum is dedicated to the work of the **Hans Memling**, one of the foremost Flemish painters of the 15th century. The museum also highlights the rich history of the hospital, which served as both a medical and religious center for centuries.

Highlights: Among the museum's treasures is Memling's famous **"The Last Judgment"** altarpiece, as well as other religious works like **"Saint Ursula's Triptych"**. The museum also provides a glimpse into the hospital's history with exhibits on medical practices from the medieval period.

What to Expect: The museum offers a well-curated collection of religious art in a historical setting. The museum's small, intimate nature allows for a focused and quiet experience.

Cost: Tickets are €10 for adults, with reduced rates for seniors and students.

Travel Tip: Be sure to check out the adjacent hospital area, which includes displays about medieval medical practices and the history of Brugge as a key center for religious pilgrimage.

3. The Frietmuseum

- **Address**: Vlamingstraat 33, 8000 Brugge
- **Phone**: +32 50 61 62 18
- **Website**: www.frietmuseum.be

While Brugge is known for its art, the **Frietmuseum** adds a lighter, fun twist to the city's cultural offerings. Dedicated to the history of the **French fry** (yes, Belgium's famous fries!), this quirky museum tells the story of one of Belgium's most beloved foods, from its origins in South America to its rise as a Belgian national dish.

Highlights: The museum includes interactive exhibits, vintage advertisements, and of course, a chance to learn about how fries are made. The museum also offers a tasting room where you can sample some of the best fries in Brugge with a variety of dipping sauces.

What to Expect: The museum is a mix of history and humor, making it perfect for those who want a light-hearted break from Brugge's more traditional art offerings.

Cost: Admission is €8 for adults, and €6 for children.

Travel Tip: Don't leave without trying the fries in the museum's restaurant. They're freshly made and paired with a variety of local sauces, a treat for both adults and kids alike.

4. Choco-Story Brugge

- **Address**: Wijnzakstraat 2, 8000 Brugge
- **Phone**: +32 50 34 12 43
- **Website**: www.choco-story.be

If you're a chocolate lover, the **Choco-Story Museum** is a must-visit. This museum focuses on the history of chocolate, from its origins in the Americas to its transformation into the sweet treat we know today. Brugge has long been famous for its chocolate, and this museum explores the city's rich tradition of chocolate making.

Highlights: The museum offers a history of chocolate-making, with displays about cocoa, chocolate craftsmanship, and the early methods of production. Visitors also get to participate in live demonstrations where you can see how chocolate is made and even taste samples.

What to Expect: The museum has interactive exhibits that appeal to all ages. From ancient Aztec recipes to Belgian pralines, you'll learn about every step of chocolate's journey. Don't forget to visit the chocolate shop at the end for some delicious souvenirs.

Cost: Admission is €10 for adults, with discounts for children and families.

Travel Tip: If you're visiting Brugge for its famous chocolate, be sure to stop by other renowned chocolate shops in the city after your visit to **Choco-Story** for the full experience.

5. Gruuthuse Museum

- **Address**: Gruuthusestraat 17, 8000 Brugge
- **Phone**: +32 50 44 87 11
- **Website**: www.museumbrugge.be

The **Gruuthuse Museum** offers a fascinating look into Brugge's history, showcasing art, furniture, tapestries, and decorative items from the Middle Ages to the 19th century. Located in a beautiful Gothic mansion, the museum is a great place to understand the luxurious lifestyle of Brugge's wealthy merchants in the past.

Highlights: The museum's collection includes religious art, sculptures, medieval furniture, and historical tapestries. The building itself is just as impressive as the exhibits, with its ornate rooms and antique furnishings. The museum also provides a look at the history of the **Gruuthuse family**, who were influential in Brugge during the 14th and 15th centuries.

What to Expect: The museum offers a variety of exhibits covering different periods, giving visitors an in-depth look at Brugge's social and cultural evolution.

Cost: Entrance is €10 for adults.

Travel Tip: The museum is often less crowded than the larger sites in Brugge, making it a great option for those seeking a more relaxed museum experience.

Exploring Brugge's Canals

One of the most scenic ways to explore Brugge is by its canals. The city's network of waterways has been an integral part of its history and has earned it the nickname "Venice of the North." You can experience these charming canals by boat or on foot, each offering a different perspective of the city's medieval beauty.

Canal Boat Tours

Exploring Brugge's canals by boat is a fantastic way to experience the city's charm and beauty. Several companies offer boat tours that will take you through the winding waterways, providing an informative and relaxing experience.

Popular Canal Boat Tour Companies:

1. Brugge Canal Tours

- Address: Rozenhoedkaai, 8000 Brugge
- Cost: **€10** for a 30-minute tour.
- **Travel Tip**: These tours are very popular, so it's best to go early in the morning or later in the evening to avoid large crowds.
- **Boottochten Brugge**
- Address: Dijver, 8000 Brugge
- Cost: **€10** for a 30-minute boat ride.
- **Travel Tip**: Ask the boat guide for information about the city's history and architecture. They often share interesting facts you might not get elsewhere.
- **What to Expect**: On these tours, you'll get to pass under charming bridges, see medieval buildings lining the canals, and catch glimpses of quiet courtyards and gardens. The tours often include a knowledgeable guide who will share historical tidbits and details about the buildings you pass.

Walking Along the Canals

For a more leisurely way to explore the canals, walking along them is just as rewarding. You can take your time to wander through Brugge's quaint streets, stopping to admire the view at various points along the water. Some of the most scenic walks include routes along **Dijver Canal** and the path near **Minnewater Park**.

- **What to Expect**: These canal-side walks are lined with historical buildings, cafes, and charming bridges. It's a great way to discover Brugge at your own pace. One of the best places to walk along the canal is **Rozenhoedkaai**, where the view of the Belfry and surrounding buildings is picture-perfect.
- **Cost**: Free to explore the canals on foot.
- **Travel Tip**: For the best photos, visit **Rozenhoedkaai** at sunset when the water reflects the buildings and the sky turns golden.

Off-the-Beaten-Path

Hidden Gems to Explore

Brugge is a city filled with well-known landmarks and tourist hotspots, but to really experience its charm, it's worth venturing off the beaten path. Brugge has plenty of hidden gems where you can escape the crowds and enjoy the authentic atmosphere of this medieval city. Here are some of the best off-the-beaten-path spots to explore in Brugge.

1. Quiet Parks and Green Spaces

Brugge is often associated with its picturesque canals and historic streets, but it also has some peaceful parks and green spaces where you can take a break from the busy city center and enjoy nature.

(I) Minnewater Park (Lake of Love)

- **Address**: Minnewaterpark, 8000 Brugge
- **Phone**: +32 50 44 87 11

Minnewater Park, also known as the **Lake of Love**, is one of the most tranquil spots in Brugge. The park is home to a beautiful lake surrounded by trees, giving it a serene atmosphere perfect for a quiet stroll or a relaxing break. It's one of those places where you can easily forget you're in the heart of the city.

What to Expect: You'll find plenty of benches by the lake, ideal for sitting and people-watching or reading a book. The park is also home to several swans, which only add to the peaceful ambiance. The **Minnewater Bridge**, an iconic red-brick bridge, provides a perfect photo opportunity.

Cost: Free to visit.

Travel Tip: The park is located just a 10-minute walk from **Brugge Station**, making it a convenient stop on your way to or from the city center.

(ii) Koningen Astridpark

- **Address**: Astridpark, 8000 Brugge
- **Phone**: +32 50 44 87 11

A lesser-known gem, **Koningen Astridpark** is located a bit further from the main tourist areas but is still within walking distance from the city center. This peaceful park is great for those who want to experience a quieter part of Brugge, away from the busy crowds.

What to Expect: The park has wide green lawns, mature trees, and a small pond, making it a perfect spot to relax or enjoy a picnic. It's often overlooked by tourists, so you'll have the place almost to yourself.

Cost: Free to visit.

Travel Tip: The park is close to the **Beguinage**, so you can combine a visit to both locations for a peaceful afternoon walk.

2. Hidden Galleries and Art Spaces

Brugge is known for its art, but many of the city's most interesting galleries are off the main tourist circuit. These smaller, lesser-known spots offer an intimate experience with the city's artistic history.

(I) St. George's Art Gallery
- **Address**: Mariastraat 10, 8000 Brugge
- **Phone**: +32 50 34 91 08
- **Website**: www.stgeorgesgallery.be

Located just off the main square, **St. George's Art Gallery** is a hidden gem for those interested in contemporary art. The gallery specializes in Belgian and European art from the **19th and 20th centuries**, and its intimate setting allows for a personal experience with each exhibit.

What to Expect: The gallery is housed in a beautiful old building and regularly features new exhibitions, often showcasing lesser-known local artists. It's a great spot for those who want to experience Brugge's art scene beyond the famous museums.

Cost: Entrance is usually **€5**, with occasional free admission during special events or openings.

Travel Tip: The gallery is small but worth the visit if you want to enjoy art in a calm and intimate environment.

(ii) Lumina Domestica
- **Address**: Ezelstraat 53, 8000 Brugge
- **Phone**: +32 50 67 03 77

- **Website**: www.lumina-domestica.be

Lumina Domestica is a unique gallery in Brugge, focusing on the fascinating world of **lighting design**. It's one of the only places in the city where you can explore the history of lighting as an art form. The gallery features works from contemporary artists who specialize in creating innovative lighting sculptures and installations.

What to Expect: The exhibits are interactive and often involve modern lighting technology to create stunning visual effects. It's a unique spot that will appeal to design lovers and those interested in how lighting can be used as an artistic medium.

Cost: Entrance is €8 for adults, with discounts for students and seniors.

Travel Tip: The gallery is located near the **Begijnhof** area, so you can easily add this visit to your day of exploring Brugge's quieter spots.

Local Shops and Unique Finds

While Brugge is filled with tourist shops selling souvenirs, there are also plenty of local shops where you can find something truly special. These stores offer a more authentic Brugge experience, whether you're looking for handcrafted goods, unique antiques, or locally produced goods.

1. The Black Swan Antiques

- **Address**: Korte Vuldersstraat 23, 8000 Brugge
- **Phone**: +32 50 34 42 61

For those who appreciate antiques and vintage items, **The Black Swan Antiques** is a must-visit. This small but fascinating store specializes in a wide range of antique pieces, from **furniture** and **china** to **old maps** and **prints**. It's perfect for those looking for unique and timeless souvenirs.

What to Expect: The store is filled with interesting and beautiful items, many of which reflect Brugge's history. You can find items from the **18th and 19th centuries**, including fine porcelain, old books, and vintage jewelry.

Cost: Prices vary widely depending on the item, but many small pieces start around **€10 to €15**.

Travel Tip: Take your time to explore the store, as you never know what hidden treasures you might find among the eclectic selection.

2. Papershop

- **Address**: Kuipersstraat 4, 8000 Brugge
- **Phone**: +32 50 34 53 39
- **Website**: www.papershopbrugge.be

If you're a fan of paper goods, **Papershop** is the place to be. This quaint shop specializes in beautiful, high-quality paper products, including **handmade notebooks**, **art prints**, and **stationery**. The shop's rustic charm and carefully curated selection make it a great spot for finding a special gift or something for yourself.

What to Expect: The store offers a variety of paper products, from colorful notebooks and cards to intricate, handcrafted items. It's a great place to find something with a local touch.

Cost: Prices start around **€5 to €10** for smaller items like cards, with notebooks and prints ranging from **€15 to €30**.

Travel Tip: If you're looking for a unique and meaningful souvenir, Papershop is the perfect place to find something that reflects Brugge's artistic and historical spirit.

3. The Chocolate Line

- **Address**: Simon Stevinplein 19, 8000 Brugge
- **Phone**: +32 50 34 10 38
- **Website**: www.thechocolateline.be

While Brugge is known for its chocolate, **The Chocolate Line** offers something truly unique. This shop is famous for its **creative and unusual chocolate creations**, which push the boundaries of what you might expect from a traditional Belgian chocolatier. From chocolate with chili to chocolate lollipops filled with champagne, this shop brings a modern twist to the classic Belgian treat.

What to Expect: You can try new and exotic chocolate combinations, all made with high-quality Belgian chocolate. The shop also offers workshops where you can learn how to create your own chocolate masterpieces.

Cost: Prices for chocolates start at **€5 to €8** for small boxes, with more elaborate creations costing upwards of **€20**.

Travel Tip: Stop by for a tasting or buy some unique chocolates as a gift or souvenir. They also offer international shipping if you fall in love with their creations.

Brugge for Families

Brugge may be known for its historic charm and romantic atmosphere, but it's also an excellent destination for families. The city offers a wide variety of kid-friendly attractions that combine fun and education in a way that both adults and children will enjoy. From interactive museums to parks and boat rides, here's a list of the best family-friendly activities and spots in Brugge.

Kid-Friendly Attractions

1. The Frietmuseum

- **Address**: Vlamingstraat 33, 8000 Brugge
- **Phone**: +32 50 61 62 18
- **Website**: www.frietmuseum.be

The **Frietmuseum** is a quirky, fun stop for families, especially with young children. This museum is dedicated to Belgium's famous fries (or **frites**), tracing their history from their origins in South America to their transformation into the beloved Belgian snack. It's educational yet entertaining, and kids will enjoy the interactive displays.

What to Expect: The museum is colorful and engaging, with plenty of hands-on exhibits. Kids can learn about the different varieties of potatoes, how fries are made, and even watch a video about the history of fries in Belgium.

Cost: €8 for adults, €6 for children aged 6-12, and free for children under 6.

Travel Tip: Don't miss the tasting area at the end, where kids can enjoy fresh fries served with a variety of sauces. It's a perfect break after exploring the museum.

2. The Choco-Story Museum

- **Address**: Wijnzakstraat 2, 8000 Brugge
- **Phone**: +32 50 34 12 43
- **Website**: www.choco-story.be

For families with sweet-toothed kids, **Choco-Story** is an unmissable experience. This chocolate museum covers the history of chocolate, from its origins in the Aztec Empire to its role in Belgian culture today. The museum is full of interactive exhibits, which make it both fun and educational.

What to Expect: Kids can enjoy live demonstrations where chocolate is made in front of them. There are also hands-on activities, such as molding your own chocolate shapes to take home. The museum even lets you taste the chocolate products along the way.

Cost: €10 for adults, €6 for children aged 6-12, and free for children under 6.

Travel Tip: Be sure to stop by the shop at the end of the museum for some high-quality Belgian chocolates to take home.

3. Burg Square and The Belfry

- **Address**: Markt, 8000 Brugge
- **Phone**: +32 50 44 46 46
- **Website**: www.belfortbrugge.be

While **Burg Square** and the **Belfry of Brugge** are iconic landmarks, they can also be fun for children. Climbing the Belfry's **366 steps** is an exciting challenge for older kids, and the panoramic views from the top are breathtaking. If your kids are a bit younger, you can still enjoy the square and explore the nearby areas.

What to Expect: The climb to the top of the Belfry can be tiring but rewarding. At the top, you'll be treated to stunning views of Brugge and its canals. Burg Square itself is great for photos, with its historic buildings and the **Basilica of the Holy Blood** nearby. The bell tower rings every 15 minutes, which kids will find fun.

Cost: **€12** for adults, **€8** for children aged 6-12.

Travel Tip: If climbing the tower sounds too much, just exploring Burg Square and the **Basilica** is still an excellent way to experience Brugge's rich history without the physical exertion.

4. Minnewater Park (Lake of Love)

- **Address**: Minnewaterpark, 8000 Brugge
- **Phone**: +32 50 44 87 11

Minnewater Park, often called the **Lake of Love**, is a peaceful and scenic park that's ideal for families looking to relax. It's one of the most beautiful spots in Brugge, with a lake surrounded by trees and swans. The park is perfect for a quiet stroll, a picnic, or simply letting the kids run around.

What to Expect: The park is known for its idyllic lake and resident swans, which children will love to watch. There are benches where you can sit and relax while kids enjoy the open space. It's also a great spot for a family picnic, especially in the warmer months.

Cost: Free to visit.

Travel Tip: The park is just a 10-minute walk from **Brugge Station**, so it's easy to reach if you're coming from the train.

5. Boat Tour of Brugge's Canals

- **Address**: Rozenhoedkaai, 8000 Brugge
- **Phone**: +32 50 34 04 90
- **Website**: www.bruggecanaltours.com

Taking a **canal boat tour** is a fun way for families to explore Brugge. It's an exciting, relaxing activity that allows kids to see the city from a unique perspective. The boat ride takes you through Brugge's historic canals, passing by stunning architecture and charming bridges.

What to Expect: The boat tours usually last about **30 minutes** and are a great way for kids to enjoy Brugge from the water. The guide will share interesting facts about the city's history, and kids will love the views of the canals lined with picturesque houses.

Cost: €10 for adults, €6 for children.

Travel Tip: The tours are popular, so it's a good idea to book your tickets in advance during peak season. It's also a great option if you need a break from walking around the city.

6. Basilica of the Holy Blood

- **Address**: Burg Square, 8000 Brugge
- **Phone**: +32 50 34 63 80
- **Website**: www.holybloodbasilica.be

For families who enjoy learning about history and culture, the **Basilica of the Holy Blood** offers a unique and fascinating experience. This small, but beautiful church is home to a vial that is said to contain drops of Christ's blood, brought back to Brugge during the Crusades.

What to Expect: The basilica is peaceful and offers a glimpse into Brugge's medieval past. The lower chapel is dark and atmospheric, while the upper chapel is where the Holy Blood relic is kept. It's an interesting stop for older children and families who enjoy learning about religious history.

Cost: €2 for adults, with free entry for children under 12.

Travel Tip: The basilica is located in **Burg Square**, which is a great area to explore afterward. Make sure to visit early to avoid crowds, as it can get busy with tourists.

7. Boudewijn Seapark

- **Address**: De Ketting 1, 8200 Brugge
- **Phone**: +32 50 39 63 00
- **Website**: www.boudewijnseapark.be

For a full day of family fun, **Boudewijn Seapark** is a fantastic option. It's a large amusement park located just outside the city center, featuring both animal attractions and thrilling rides. Kids will love the dolphin and sea lion shows, and there are also plenty of rides and play areas for all ages.

What to Expect: In addition to animal shows, the park has a wide range of rides suitable for younger children and teens alike. There's also a water park section with slides and a wave pool for when the weather is warm.

Cost: Tickets start at **€20** for children and **€25** for adults, with discounts for families.

Travel Tip: If you're visiting in the summer, be sure to bring swimwear for the water park section. The park is located about **15 minutes by car** from the city center, so it's easily accessible.

Romantic Activities for Couples

Love-Filled Activities

Brugge, with its canals, cobbled streets, and stunning architecture, is an incredibly romantic destination. If you're on a honeymoon, celebrating an anniversary, or just looking for a romantic getaway, Brugge offers a variety of activities that are perfect for couples. From intimate strolls along the canals to cozy boat rides, here are some of the best romantic activities you can enjoy in this fairy-tale city.

1. Stroll Along the Canals

One of the most romantic things you can do in Brugge is to take a leisurely walk along the city's canals. With the gentle sound of water flowing and the historic buildings reflecting in the canals, these walks offer an intimate experience and some of the best photo opportunities in the city.

(I) **Dijver Canal**: This canal is one of the most picturesque in Brugge, with beautiful old houses lining its banks. Stroll hand in hand while admiring the views of the **Belfry Tower** and the **Minnewater** (Lake of Love).

(ii) **Rozenhoedkaai**: This is one of the most iconic spots for couples, offering a romantic view of the canals, medieval buildings, and the **Belfry of Brugge**.

It's a great spot to pause for a photo or simply enjoy the peaceful atmosphere.

Cost: Free to explore.

Travel Tip: If you're visiting during the quieter hours, early in the morning or later in the evening, you'll avoid crowds and get a more serene experience.

2. Take a Boat Ride Through the Canals

Exploring Brugge's canals by boat is one of the most romantic ways to see the city. The boat tours provide a unique perspective of the city, passing by charming buildings, hidden courtyards, and under beautiful bridges.

Boat Tour Companies:

(I) Brugge Canal Tours

- Address: Rozenhoedkaai, 8000 Brugge
- Phone: +32 50 34 04 90
- Cost: **€10** for a 30-minute ride.
- **Travel Tip**: Book a boat ride in the late afternoon to enjoy the soft light and tranquil atmosphere. If you're looking for something a bit more private, consider renting a boat for just the two of you, which allows you to set your own pace.

(ii) Boottochten Brugge

- Address: Dijver, 8000 Brugge
- Phone: +32 50 34 48 92
- Cost: **€10** for a 30-minute tour.
- **Travel Tip**: For a romantic twist, try the evening boat tours when the city's lights reflect off the water for an enchanting experience.

3. Visit the Belfry of Brugge

While the **Belfry of Brugge** is a popular tourist attraction, it's also a great spot for couples looking for breathtaking views of the city. Climb the **366 steps** together to the top of the bell tower, where you'll be rewarded with a panoramic view of Brugge and its beautiful surroundings.

- **Address**: Markt, 8000 Brugge
- **Phone**: +32 50 44 46 46
- **Cost**: €12 for adults, with discounts available for students and children.
- **Travel Tip**: Climbing the Belfry can be a fun and challenging experience for couples. Arrive early in the morning or late in the evening to avoid the crowds and enjoy a more intimate visit.

4. Romantic Dinner at Intimate Restaurants

Brugge is home to many intimate restaurants that offer romantic settings for a perfect evening out. Whether you're looking for traditional Belgian cuisine or a more modern dining experience, the city has something for every couple.

(I) De Karmeliet

- Address: Langestraat 19, 8000 Brugge
- Phone: +32 50 34 23 40
- Website: www.restaurantdekarmeliet.com
- This Michelin-starred restaurant offers a refined atmosphere and exquisite dishes. The intimate ambiance makes it perfect for couples celebrating a special occasion.
- **Cost**: Expect to pay around **€100 to €150** per person for a multi-course dinner, excluding wine.

(ii) Bistro de Schie

- Address: Schie 12, 8000 Brugge
- Phone: +32 50 34 34 64
- This cozy bistro offers a more relaxed atmosphere with a fantastic selection of Belgian dishes. It's perfect for a quiet and intimate dinner away from the crowds.
- **Cost**: Main courses range from **€15 to €25**.

(iii) De Vlaamsche Pot

- Address: Stoofstraat 8, 8000 Brugge
- Phone: +32 50 34 32 50
- This traditional Flemish restaurant offers a cozy and intimate setting, perfect for a romantic evening. The hearty **stoofvlees** (beef stew) and **moules-frites** (mussels and fries) are must-tries.
- **Cost**: Main courses typically range from **€18 to €30**.
- **Travel Tip**: For a truly intimate dining experience, try to reserve a table by the window, so you can enjoy the view of Brugge's canals or cobblestone streets while you dine.

5. Sunset at Minnewater Park (Lake of Love)

Another romantic spot in Brugge is **Minnewater Park**. Known as the **Lake of Love**, it's an idyllic location for couples who want to take in the beauty of nature and enjoy a peaceful afternoon or evening. The park is especially stunning at sunset when the light hits the lake and the surrounding trees.

- **Address**: Minnewaterpark, 8000 Brugge
- **Phone**: +32 50 44 87 11
- **Cost**: Free to visit.
- **Travel Tip**: Bring a blanket and some snacks for a romantic picnic by the lake. You can also take a boat ride on the lake, adding to the experience of being surrounded by nature.

6. Horse-Drawn Carriage Ride

For a classic and romantic experience, take a **horse-drawn carriage ride** through Brugge's historic streets. This is a relaxing and charming way to see the city's most famous landmarks while cuddling up with your partner. The ride takes you through the cobblestone streets, past historic buildings, and through some of Brugge's picturesque neighborhoods.

- **Address**: Markt Square, 8000 Brugge
- **Phone**: +32 50 34 42 42
- **Cost**: Around €40 for a 30-minute ride.
- **Travel Tip**: This is a great way to see Brugge if you want to rest your feet and enjoy the beauty of the city in a more intimate setting.

7. Climb the Minnewater Bridge

The **Minnewater Bridge** is another beautiful spot for couples to enjoy a romantic moment. The bridge spans the canal near **Minnewater Park** and offers a picturesque view of the lake, making it one of the most iconic spots in Brugge. The area around the bridge is perfect for a quiet, intimate walk, with the swans gliding across the lake and the trees providing plenty of shade.

- **Address**: Minnewaterpark, 8000 Brugge
- **Cost**: Free to visit.
- **Travel Tip**: Visit at sunset for the best views and an extra romantic atmosphere.

8. Evening Canal Walk

Another romantic way to experience Brugge is by taking an **evening canal walk**. Brugge's canals are magical when the lights from the buildings and bridges reflect off the water. The soft glow of the city at night creates a serene and romantic ambiance, perfect for a quiet walk with your loved one.

- **What to Expect**: The canals are well-lit in the evening, making it safe to walk along the water after dark. Some of the most romantic areas to explore include **Dijver Canal** and **Rozenhoedkaai**, which are known for their stunning reflections.
- **Cost**: Free to walk.
- **Travel Tip**: If you're staying in Brugge for several days, take a canal walk at different times of day to see how the light changes the atmosphere.

9. Romantic Photoshoot in Brugge

Brugge offers plenty of opportunities for couples to capture memories together, whether it's in front of the **Belfry Tower**, by the canals, or in the peaceful parks. Many local photographers offer **romantic photoshoots**, where they will take you to the most picturesque spots in the city, creating beautiful images that you'll cherish forever.

- **What to Expect**: A professional photographer will guide you to some of Brugge's most iconic spots, taking natural and posed shots that capture your love and the beauty of the city.
- **Cost**: Prices typically start around **€150** for a 1-hour photoshoot, depending on the photographer and the package.
- **Travel Tip**: Book a session early in the day or late in the afternoon for the best lighting and fewer crowds.

Entertainment and Nightlife

Best Bars and Pubs

Brugge may be known for its medieval charm and canals, but it also offers a great selection of bars and pubs for those looking to enjoy the nightlife. If you're into tasting Belgian beers or simply soaking up the local atmosphere, Brugge has plenty of cozy spots that cater to all kinds of drinkers.

1. De Halve Maan Brewery

- **Address**: Walplein 26, 8000 Brugge
- **Phone**: +32 50 34 73 53
- **Website**: www.halvemaan.be

For those wanting to experience the true taste of Brugge's beer culture, **De Halve Maan Brewery** is a must-visit. Not only is it one of Brugge's oldest breweries, but it also offers an authentic atmosphere where you can enjoy their signature beers, including **Brugse Zot** and **Straffe Hendrik**. The brewery is located along the canal, adding to the charm of the experience.

What to Expect: You can enjoy a cold pint in the brewery's bar or even take a guided tour to learn about the beer-making process while sampling different brews.

Cost: A pint of beer costs around **€3 to €5**.

Travel Tip: Don't miss the chance to try their exclusive **Straffe Hendrik** beer, which is a local favorite.

2. The Beerwall

- **Address**: Sint-Jakobsstraat 20, 8000 Brugge
- **Phone**: +32 50 34 14 57
- **Website**: www.thebeerwall.be

If you're a beer enthusiast, **The Beerwall** is a great place to try out a variety of Belgian beers. This laid-back bar offers a wide selection of local and international brews, with a special focus on Belgian craft beers. With its rustic décor and cozy atmosphere, it's a perfect place for a night out with friends or a relaxed evening.

What to Expect: A large selection of **Belgian beers** from local breweries, including rare finds and specialty brews. The bar is known for its **beer wall**, which displays a huge variety of beers available on tap.

Cost: Beers range from **€3 to €6**, depending on the type and size.

Travel Tip: The bar has a great selection of snacks and appetizers, so make sure to pair your beer with some traditional Belgian bites.

3. 't Brugs Beertje

- **Address**: Kemelstraat 5, 8000 Brugge
- **Phone**: +32 50 34 39 80
- **Website**: www.brugsbeertje.be

If you're looking for a cozy, old-fashioned pub with a local touch, **'t Brugs Beertje** is the place to be. This small and intimate bar offers over 300 different Belgian beers, making it one of Brugge's top spots for beer lovers. The atmosphere is warm and welcoming, and the knowledgeable staff can help guide you to the perfect beer to suit your taste.

What to Expect: A traditional Belgian pub with wooden beams, a small but inviting space, and a huge selection of local beers. The bar serves a mix of classic beers and unique, hard-to-find brews from small Belgian craft breweries.

Cost: Beer prices range from **€3 to €5**.

Travel Tip: Ask the bartender for a recommendation based on your tastes. They're happy to help you discover new beers.

4. Café Rose Red

- **Address**: Vlamingstraat 10, 8000 Brugge
- **Phone**: +32 50 34 02 73

For a relaxed, no-frills pub with a historic feel, **Café Rose Red** is a popular choice among locals and visitors alike. This cozy bar is located in the heart of Brugge and is perfect for those who enjoy a laid-back vibe with a good beer selection.

What to Expect: A simple yet inviting atmosphere, ideal for enjoying a drink after a day of sightseeing. The bar serves a variety of Belgian beers, and the décor gives a glimpse into Brugge's past.

Cost: A typical beer will set you back around **€2 to €4**.

Travel Tip: Café Rose Red is a great place to grab a quick drink before heading out to see more of Brugge's nightlife. The bar is popular with both tourists and locals, so it can get busy in the evening.

Live Music Venues and Events

Brugge may be known for its medieval history, but the city also has a vibrant live music scene that caters to a variety of tastes. From jazz to contemporary and folk, there are plenty of spots where you can enjoy live performances and immerse yourself in Brugge's cultural side.

1. De Werf

- **Address**: Predikherenrei 1, 8000 Brugge
- **Phone**: +32 50 34 93 79
- **Website**: www.dewerf.be

De Werf is Brugge's leading venue for live music, with performances ranging from jazz and folk to electronic and experimental music. This modern, artsy venue hosts concerts, festivals, and events throughout the year, making it a must-visit for music lovers. Whether you're a fan of local bands or international acts, De Werf offers a space for all kinds of performances.

What to Expect: A variety of live performances, including both local and international artists. The venue is known for its intimate atmosphere, where you can get close to the stage and enjoy an up-close musical experience.

Cost: Ticket prices vary depending on the event, typically ranging from **€10 to €30**.

Travel Tip: Check their website for the latest events and concerts. De Werf often holds smaller gigs, so it's a great place to discover new talent.

2. Café de Zwarte Linde

- **Address**: Langestraat 12, 8000 Brugge
- **Phone**: +32 50 34 34 14

For a more intimate, cozy venue, **Café de Zwarte Linde** offers a great atmosphere with live music on the weekends. The café hosts acoustic performances, jazz, and local bands, offering a laid-back environment where you can enjoy good music and drinks.

What to Expect: A relaxed setting where you can listen to live music in a casual environment. The café is small but charming, with a good selection of Belgian beers and an inviting ambiance.

Cost: Entrance is often free, but some performances may require a small cover charge (around **€5 to €10**).

Travel Tip: The café is small, so try to arrive early if you want to grab a good seat. The intimate setting makes it a great spot for couples or friends.

3. Concertgebouw Brugge

- **Address**: 't Zand 34, 8000 Brugge
- **Phone**: +32 50 47 69 99
- **Website**: www.concertgebouw.be

For those who enjoy larger, more formal performances, **Concertgebouw Brugge** is the go-to venue for classical, jazz, and contemporary music. The concert hall is one of the best in Belgium, offering a world-class setting for musical performances. While it's mainly known for classical concerts, the venue also hosts pop, jazz, and world music events.

What to Expect: A variety of performances, from full orchestras to smaller jazz bands. The acoustics are excellent, making it a great place to see top-tier performers.

Cost: Tickets generally range from **€15 to €50**, depending on the performance.

Travel Tip: Check their calendar for performances during your visit. The venue is a short walk from **Burg Square**, so it's easy to combine a show with a visit to the city's historic center.

4. Jazzcafé 't Zwart Huis

- **Address**: Kuipersstraat 23, 8000 Brugge
- **Phone**: +32 50 34 26 87
- **Website**: www.jazzcafe.be

For jazz lovers, **Jazzcafé 't Zwart Huis** is the perfect venue. This cozy café hosts live jazz performances on weekends, featuring both local talent and international artists. It's a great spot to enjoy some good music in a relaxed, intimate setting.

What to Expect: A laid-back atmosphere with great live jazz. The café has an old-school feel with a modern twist, offering a perfect environment for a night out with friends or a date.

Cost: Entry is free, but expect a small cover charge for special performances (around **€5 to €10**).

Travel Tip: Arrive early to get a seat, especially if there's a popular band performing. The café can get packed, especially on weekend nights.

Cinemas, Nightclubs, and Dance Spots

Theatrical Shows and Cinemas

B rugge may be known for its historical charm, but it also has a thriving cultural scene. From cinematic experiences showcasing Belgian talent to theatrical performances, there are several venues where visitors can immerse themselves in Brugge's arts and entertainment.

1. Cinema Lumière

- **Address**: Sint-Jakobsstraat 20, 8000 Brugge
- **Phone**: +32 50 33 11 80
- **Website**: www.cinemalumiere.be

For those looking to catch a movie, **Cinema Lumière** is one of the top spots in Brugge. This independent cinema screens a mix of Belgian, European, and international films, with a special focus on arthouse cinema and documentaries. It's the ideal place for movie lovers who want to experience something different from the usual Hollywood blockbusters.

What to Expect: Cinema Lumière is a cozy venue with multiple screening rooms, offering both new releases and classic films. The cinema is known for showing films in their original language with Dutch or French subtitles, providing an authentic viewing experience for international audiences.

Cost: Ticket prices are generally around €10 for adults and €8 for students.

Travel Tip: Check their website for the weekly schedule, as they often host special film events, like **film festivals** or **Belgian film nights**, showcasing local talent.

2. Stadsschouwburg Brugge

- **Address**: Vlamingstraat 29, 8000 Brugge
- **Phone**: +32 50 44 46 81
- **Website**: www.stadsschouwburgbrugge.be

For those interested in live theatrical performances, **Stadsschouwburg Brugge** is the city's primary venue for plays, musicals, and cultural shows. The venue hosts a wide range of performances throughout the year, from traditional Belgian theater to contemporary acts, and even international touring productions.

What to Expect: The **Stadsschouwburg** offers a rich cultural experience, with performances by both Belgian and international theater companies. It's the place to see theatrical plays, operas, comedy shows, and sometimes even live dance performances. The venue also hosts film screenings, particularly for Belgian cinema.

Cost: Tickets for performances typically range from €15 to €40, depending on the show.

Travel Tip: If you're interested in local theater, try to catch a performance in **Dutch or French** for an authentic experience. English-friendly performances are available from time to time, so check their schedule.

3. Cinema Nova Brugge

- **Address**: Nieuwstraat 35, 8000 Brugge
- **Phone**: +32 50 34 47 40
- **Website**: www.cinemanova.be

Cinema Nova Brugge is another excellent venue for those who love independent films. It's an intimate cinema that prides itself on screening lesser-known Belgian films and international releases. The cinema is popular with locals and offers an alternative to the larger commercial cinemas in Brugge.

What to Expect: Expect to find a variety of films from different genres, often focusing on **local Belgian talent** and international cinema that doesn't always get a wide release. Cinema Nova Brugge is also known for screening **film retrospectives** and hosting **movie discussions** after screenings.

Cost: Tickets cost around **€9** for adults, with discounts for students or seniors.

Travel Tip: Cinema Nova Brugge is located in the heart of the city, making it a great place to visit after a day of sightseeing. They also offer special deals for **film lovers**, so be sure to check their calendar for events.

Nightclubs and Dance Spots

Brugge might not have the same intense nightlife scene as larger cities, but it still offers some great spots for dancing and enjoying a night out.

1. Café de Rots

- **Address**: Wijnzakstraat 25, 8000 Brugge

CINEMAS, NIGHTCLUBS, AND DANCE SPOTS

- **Phone**: +32 50 34 27 50
- **Website**: www.cafederots.be

For those looking for a casual yet lively spot to dance and enjoy the night, **Café de Rots** is one of Brugge's top choices. This popular bar and nightclub hosts regular events, including live DJ sets, themed parties, and local performances. It's a fun spot to hang out with friends and meet other travelers.

What to Expect: Expect a mix of **dance music**, **house**, **techno**, and **pop**. The club has a vibrant crowd, and it's a great place to dance and let loose. The venue is quite intimate but always filled with energy. They often host themed nights, so be sure to check their schedule.

Cost: Cover charge varies depending on the night, generally between **€5 and €10**.

Travel Tip: The club tends to get crowded on weekends, so arrive early to avoid waiting in line.

2. De Republiek

- **Address**: Zilverstraat 7, 8000 Brugge
- **Phone**: +32 50 34 37 10
- **Website**: www.republiek.be

De Republiek is one of the more upscale nightclubs in Brugge, with a sleek, modern design and a more sophisticated vibe. It's popular for its electronic music and DJ nights, drawing a crowd that loves to dance into the early hours.

What to Expect: The club plays a mix of **house, electronic**, and **techno music**, with international and local DJs taking to the decks on weekends. The venue is stylish and provides a great setting for an energetic night of dancing.

Cost: Expect to pay around **€8 to €12** for entry, with special events or guest DJs having a slightly higher cover charge.

Travel Tip: If you're looking for a more upmarket night out with quality sound and an energetic crowd, De Republiek is a solid choice. The club also has VIP areas, so you can book a table for an exclusive experience.

3. The Public

- **Address**: Steenstraat 13, 8000 Brugge
- **Phone**: +32 50 34 64 66
- **Website**: www.thepublicbrugge.be

If you're looking for a night of dancing and fun, **The Public** is one of the best spots in Brugge for an exciting club experience. This nightclub is known for its **electronic music** and hosts regular events featuring local and international DJs.

What to Expect: A great atmosphere, with a crowd of people ready to dance and enjoy the music. The music selection includes house, deep house, and techno, offering a great beat for dancing the night away. The venue also organizes themed parties, which are a hit among locals and visitors alike.

Cost: Entry is typically **€8 to €12**, depending on the event.

Travel Tip: The club can get packed on weekends, so make sure to check out the event schedule and arrive early for the best experience.

4. Bistro De Schie

- **Address**: Schie 12, 8000 Brugge
- **Phone**: +32 50 34 34 64

Though not exactly a nightclub, **Bistro De Schie** is a perfect spot to start your night out with some drinks and light entertainment. This lively bistro and bar often has live music performances, making it a great place to kick off the evening before heading to a club or dance spot.

What to Expect: Live music events featuring local bands or solo performances, ranging from folk to pop music. The atmosphere is relaxed, making it a great place for couples or groups of friends to enjoy a drink before hitting the dance floors.

Cost: Drinks range from **€3 to €6**, and some events may have a cover charge of **€5 to €8**.

Travel Tip: If you're looking for a casual spot with live music and a friendly crowd, this is a good choice before you head out to more energetic venues.

Local Festivals and Events

Brugge is a city that knows how to celebrate, offering a wide range of festivals and events throughout the year. From religious processions to lively music festivals and cultural celebrations, Brugge has something for everyone. Here are some of the most notable festivals and events to look out for in 2025.

1. **Procession of the Holy Blood**
   - **Date**: May 21, 2025 (Ascension Day)
   - **Location**: Starts at Burg Square, Brugge
   - **Phone**: +32 50 44 46 81
   - **Website**: www.holybloodprocession.be

The **Procession of the Holy Blood** is one of Brugge's most significant and colorful events, celebrating the city's religious history. Held annually on Ascension Day, this historic procession has been taking place since the 13th century and is a fascinating mix of religious devotion, medieval pageantry, and local tradition. The procession features over 1,500 participants, including locals dressed in historical costumes, religious figures, and musicians.

What to Expect: The procession begins at **Burg Square**, where participants gather before parading through the city's cobblestone streets. The highlight of the event is the carrying of the **Relic of the Holy Blood**, a vial believed to contain drops of Christ's blood. The route is lined with crowds of spectators, and the atmosphere is both festive and reverent.

Cost: Free to watch, though seating in certain areas may be available for a fee.

Travel Tip: Arrive early to secure a good spot along the procession route, as it can get crowded, especially around **Burg Square**. Make sure to wear comfortable shoes for the walk if you're planning to follow the procession through the streets.

2. Brugge Beer Festival

- **Date**: February 2025 (exact dates TBD)
- **Location**: Beursplein, Brugge
- **Phone**: +32 50 34 80 50
- **Website**: www.bruggebeerfestival.be

Belgium's beer culture is famous worldwide, and **the Brugge Beer Festival** is the perfect way to experience this part of the country's heritage. Held every year, the festival features a wide range of Belgian craft beers from over 70 breweries. It's a great event for beer lovers, whether you're a seasoned enthusiast or new to the world of Belgian brews.

What to Expect: The festival takes place indoors at **Beursplein** and offers an impressive selection of Belgian beers, including local Brugge brews. There are tastings, workshops, and opportunities to meet the brewers themselves. You'll also find food stalls offering traditional Belgian snacks to pair with your beers.

Cost: Entrance typically costs around **€15 to €20**, which includes a tasting glass. Beer tokens are available for purchase at the venue.

Travel Tip: The festival tends to get busy, especially on the weekends, so consider going early or during a weekday session if you prefer a more relaxed experience.

3. Brugge Triennale

- **Date**: May to September 2025 (every three years)
- **Location**: Various locations throughout Brugge
- **Phone**: +32 50 44 87 11
- **Website**: www.bruggetriennale.be

The **Brugge Triennale** is a contemporary art festival that happens every three years, and 2025 will be the year for the next edition. The festival transforms Brugge into a vast open-air museum, with temporary art installations, sculptures, and exhibitions set up in various locations around the city. It's a wonderful opportunity to explore Brugge through the lens of modern art.

What to Expect: The Triennale brings together local and international artists who create innovative pieces that are displayed in public spaces across Brugge. You'll find art installations in parks, along the canals, and in historic buildings. Some installations interact with the city's architecture, creating an exciting contrast between the old and the new.

Cost: Entrance to many of the exhibitions is free, though some specific installations or events may require a ticket, typically ranging from **€5 to €15**.

Travel Tip: The installations are spread out across the city, so plan to spend a few days exploring the different pieces. The Triennale is also a great way to see parts of Brugge you might otherwise miss, like hidden courtyards and quieter neighborhoods.

4. Brugge Festival of Flanders
- **Date**: July and August 2025
- **Location**: Various venues across Brugge
- **Phone**: +32 50 47 69 99
- **Website**: www.festivaldovlaanderenbrugge.be

The **Brugge Festival of Flanders** is one of the highlights of Brugge's summer cultural calendar. This month-long festival features performances of classical music, opera, ballet, jazz, and contemporary music. The festival takes place at various venues across the city, including the **Concertgebouw Brugge**, one of the best concert halls in Belgium.

What to Expect: The festival program includes performances by renowned international artists and ensembles, as well as local Belgian talent. If you're a fan of classical music, opera, or contemporary jazz, you'll find plenty to enjoy. The festival also features outdoor concerts and performances in iconic locations, such as the **Belfry Tower** and **Market Square**.

Cost: Tickets vary depending on the performance, typically ranging from €10 to €50.

Travel Tip: Make sure to book your tickets early, as many performances sell out quickly. If you want a more intimate experience, try attending one of the smaller chamber music concerts, which offer great acoustics and a cozy atmosphere.

5. Brugge's Christmas Market and Ice Sculpture Festival
- **Date**: November 2025 to January 2026
- **Location**: Market Square, Brugge

- **Phone**: +32 50 44 87 11
- **Website**: www.christmasinbrugge.be

Brugge's **Christmas Market** is a winter wonderland, attracting visitors from around the world. The market, held annually from late November through January, takes place in **Market Square**, where you'll find over 30 stalls selling everything from handmade crafts to delicious local foods. The ice rink and the **Ice Sculpture Festival** are also part of the festivities, making it a perfect event for families and couples.

What to Expect: The Christmas Market is a cozy, festive event with twinkling lights, seasonal treats, and plenty of mulled wine to keep you warm. The **Ice Sculpture Festival** features stunning sculptures created by international artists, made entirely of ice and snow. The displays change every year, and the intricate designs are a true spectacle.

Cost: The Christmas Market is free to wander, but there is an entry fee for the **Ice Sculpture Festival**, typically **€8 to €12**.

Travel Tip: The Christmas Market gets busy in the evenings, so consider visiting earlier in the day for a quieter experience. Be sure to try some **Belgian waffles** or **frites** while you're there.

6. **Brugge's Open Air Theater (Zomeropera)**
   - **Date**: July 2025
   - **Location**: Various outdoor locations in Brugge
   - **Phone**: +32 50 47 69 99
   - **Website**: www.zomeropera.be

The **Zomeropera** (Summer Opera) is an open-air theater festival that takes place in Brugge every summer. It's a wonderful way to enjoy opera in a relaxed, outdoor setting. The festival features both traditional and contemporary operas, performed by talented musicians and opera singers. The venues for these performances include historic buildings, gardens, and even the beautiful **Minnewater Park**.

What to Expect: A mix of performances under the stars, with a relaxed atmosphere perfect for a romantic evening or a family outing. The festival includes both famous opera works and lesser-known pieces, offering a wide range of musical styles.

Cost: Tickets typically range from **€20 to €40** for adults, with discounts for students and families.

Travel Tip: Bring a blanket or a comfortable chair if you plan to attend one of the performances in a park or outdoor location, as seating can be limited.

Shopping in Brugge

Local Souvenirs

Brugge is famous for its lace-making tradition, its mouth-watering chocolate, and a variety of artisanal crafts that make excellent souvenirs. Here are the best places to shop for these traditional Brugge treasures.

1. Bruges Lace Shop

- **Address**: Heilige Geeststraat 7, 8000 Brugge
- **Phone**: +32 50 34 31 26
- **Website**: www.brugeslace.com

Lace is one of Brugge's most iconic crafts, with a history that dates back to the 16th century. The **Bruges Lace Shop** is one of the best places in the city to purchase authentic lace products. The shop sells beautifully handcrafted lace items, from delicate tablecloths to intricate doilies, as well as lace shawls and scarves.

What to Expect: The shop offers a wide variety of lace items, all made by skilled local artisans. You'll find both traditional designs and more contemporary styles. It's the perfect place to pick up a piece of Brugge's heritage.

Cost: Prices for lace items start at around €20 for smaller pieces like handkerchiefs, with larger items such as tablecloths priced upwards of €50 to €150.

Travel Tip: If you're interested in the lace-making process, check the shop's schedule for demonstrations or workshops. It's a great way to learn about this unique craft.

2. Choco-Story Brugge

- **Address**: Wijnzakstraat 2, 8000 Brugge
- **Phone**: +32 50 34 12 43
- **Website**: www.choco-story.be

Belgium is world-famous for its chocolate, and Brugge is no exception. **Choco-Story Brugge** is the perfect spot to purchase high-quality Belgian chocolates. Whether you're a fan of dark, milk, or white chocolate, this shop offers a wide selection of handmade treats that make perfect souvenirs.

What to Expect: The shop sells a variety of Belgian chocolates, from classic pralines to creative chocolate sculptures. You can also visit the museum section to learn about the history of chocolate and how it is made.

Cost: Prices for chocolate vary depending on the selection. Small boxes of pralines start at around €10, with larger gift boxes priced at €20 to €50.

Travel Tip: Choco-Story also has chocolate workshops where you can make your own chocolate treats. It's a fun, interactive way to learn about the art of chocolate-making.

3. De Halve Maan Brewery Shop

- **Address**: Walplein 26, 8000 Brugge

- **Phone**: +32 50 34 73 53
- **Website**: www.halvemaan.be

For beer lovers, **De Halve Maan Brewery** offers some of the finest Belgian brews, and the brewery shop is the best place to purchase locally brewed beer. The brewery is home to the famous **Brugse Zot** and **Straffe Hendrik**, beers that are closely associated with Brugge's beer-making tradition.

What to Expect: The shop sells De Halve Maan's signature beers, as well as merchandise like glasses, T-shirts, and beer-related accessories. You can also pick up special edition beers and limited releases.

Cost: Bottles of **Brugse Zot** start at around €2.50 for a 330ml bottle, while larger gift sets can cost between **€10 and €25**.

Travel Tip: Consider buying a gift set that includes both the beer and a branded glass, making it a great gift or souvenir.

4. Handmade in Brugge

- **Address**: Molenbeekstraat 13, 8000 Brugge
- **Phone**: +32 50 34 21 14

Handmade in Brugge is a shop that specializes in Belgian crafts and artisanal goods, offering an array of beautifully crafted items, from pottery to textiles. It's a great place to find unique souvenirs that reflect Brugge's craftsmanship.

What to Expect: The shop offers handmade ceramics, locally woven textiles, hand-blown glass, and other artisanal crafts. These items make thoughtful gifts and souvenirs, as they are both functional and beautiful.

Cost: Prices vary, but you can expect to pay **€15 to €40** for smaller handcrafted items like pottery and **€50 to €150** for larger pieces like woven blankets or glassware.

Travel Tip: The items here are often one-of-a-kind, so if you're looking for something truly special, this is the place to shop.

Best Shops for Antiques and Collectibles

For visitors looking to purchase something more unique or historical, Brugge offers a selection of antique shops and collectible stores where you can find treasures from the past. These stores are perfect for those interested in antiques, vintage goods, or rare collectibles.

1. Antiek De Ruyver

- **Address**: Noordzandstraat 38, 8000 Brugge
- **Phone**: +32 50 34 89 23

Antiek De Ruyver is a well-established antique store in Brugge, offering a wide variety of collectibles, from **antique furniture** to **fine art** and **vintage silver**. The store is known for its carefully curated collection of items that reflect Brugge's rich history.

What to Expect: You'll find a selection of antiques ranging from 18th-century furniture to vintage Belgian artworks, old mirrors, and other historical treasures. If you're a collector, this shop is a goldmine for rare and unique items.

Cost: Prices vary widely depending on the item, but expect to pay from **€50 to €200** for smaller antiques and **€500 and up** for larger pieces like furniture or fine art.

Travel Tip: If you're looking for something specific, let the shopkeeper know—they're very knowledgeable and can help you find the perfect item.

2. Sparrow Antiques

- **Address**: Noordzandstraat 5, 8000 Brugge
- **Phone**: +32 50 34 14 36

Sparrow Antiques is a charming antique shop located in the heart of Brugge. The store specializes in a variety of vintage and antique goods, including **old books**, **vintage jewelry**, and **collectible glassware**. If you're looking for something unique, this shop is an excellent place to browse.

What to Expect: The store offers an eclectic mix of antique items, including **fine jewelry**, **porcelain figurines**, and **rare books**. If you're looking for something quirky or unique, you'll find plenty of options here.

Cost: Prices range from **€15** for smaller collectibles to **€300+** for higher-end items like antique jewelry or rare books.

Travel Tip: If you're an avid collector, ask the owner about any upcoming auctions or special events—they often have exclusive items that aren't displayed in the shop.

3. Brugge Antiques

- **Address**: Vlamingstraat 34, 8000 Brugge
- **Phone**: +32 50 34 38 12

Brugge Antiques is one of the best places to find historical treasures in the city. This shop is known for its wide selection of **vintage furniture**, **art prints**, and **collectible home décor** items, offering a glimpse into the past.

What to Expect: The shop specializes in both **high-quality antiques** and **vintage items**. You'll find everything from **elegant mirrors** to **oil paintings** and **vintage home furnishings**. Many of the items have a distinct Belgian or European flair.

Cost: Items here can range from **€50 to €200** for smaller pieces to **€500+** for rare antiques or vintage furniture.

Travel Tip: If you're interested in European antiques, ask about their **period pieces**—the shop often carries furniture and art from past centuries that reflect Belgium's long history.

Designer Stores and Street Fairs

Boutiques, Fashion, and Designer Stores

Brugge is a city known for its history, but it's also home to a vibrant shopping scene, especially for those with an eye for fashion and design. The city boasts an array of stylish boutiques, high-end designer stores, and fashion-forward shops that showcase the latest trends in Belgian design.

1. Oona

- **Address**: Noordzandstraat 3, 8000 Brugge
- **Phone**: +32 50 33 29 79
- **Website**: www.oona.be

For contemporary, stylish fashion that combines classic Belgian design with modern trends, **Oona** is a must-visit. This chic boutique offers clothing from both local and international designers, specializing in high-quality fabrics and minimalist styles. You'll find items that are perfect for creating a fashionable and timeless wardrobe.

What to Expect: Expect to find fashion-forward clothing for both men and women, including high-end Belgian designers like **Essentiel Antwerp** and **A.F.**

Vandevorst. The store also features accessories, shoes, and handbags that add a sophisticated touch to any outfit.

Cost: Prices for clothing start at around **€50** for smaller accessories, with clothing items ranging from **€100 to €300**.

Travel Tip: The boutique also carries contemporary homeware, making it a great place to shop for unique, stylish items to take home.

2. Hof de Molen

- **Address**: Molenbeekstraat 9, 8000 Brugge
- **Phone**: +32 50 34 84 94

Hof de Molen is a trendy shop that offers a curated selection of clothing, accessories, and home goods by Belgian designers. Known for its mix of elegance and functionality, this boutique features a blend of cutting-edge fashion and tasteful home décor.

What to Expect: You'll find Belgian designs that are perfect for those who want high-quality, unique pieces. The store focuses on eco-friendly and sustainable products, so it's ideal for fashion-conscious shoppers who care about the environment. You can find everything from **women's fashion** to **home textiles** and accessories.

Cost: Prices for fashion items typically range from **€80 to €200**, while home goods like cushions, ceramics, and candles are priced between **€20 to €60**.

Travel Tip: The boutique is known for its welcoming atmosphere, and the staff is happy to offer styling advice or help you find the perfect gift.

3. Maison Degand

- **Address**: Simon Stevinplein 17, 8000 Brugge
- **Phone**: +32 50 34 23 67
- **Website**: www.maisondegand.com

If you're looking for high-end Belgian fashion, **Maison Degand** is the place to go. This designer boutique offers a selection of luxury brands, both Belgian and international, with a focus on timeless, elegant pieces that never go out of style.

What to Expect: Expect to find premium clothing from top Belgian designers, including **Dries Van Noten**, **Ann Demeulemeester**, and **Haider Ackermann**. The boutique also carries high-end accessories, shoes, and fragrances.

Cost: Prices for designer clothing start around **€200** for more casual items and can go up to **€1,000+** for premium designer pieces.

Travel Tip: If you're seeking a high-end shopping experience in Brugge, Maison Degand offers a refined atmosphere, where you can shop for timeless luxury items that reflect Belgian craftsmanship.

4. Lederwaren De Block

- **Address**: Hoogstraat 25, 8000 Brugge
- **Phone**: +32 50 34 16 99
- **Website**: www.deblocklederwaren.be

For high-quality leather goods, **Lederwaren De Block** is the place to go. This long-established family-run business specializes in handcrafted leather bags, belts, and wallets, all made from the finest materials.

What to Expect: The store features a wide range of leather accessories, including handbags, wallets, and belts, all made from soft, durable leather. They also offer custom-made products, so you can get a truly one-of-a-kind leather item.

Cost: Prices for leather accessories range from **€40 to €200**, depending on the item.

Travel Tip: If you're looking for a high-quality souvenir, a leather bag from **De Block** is a great choice. The shop's selection is practical, stylish, and built to last.

Brugge's Markets and Street Fairs

Brugge offers a variety of outdoor markets and street fairs throughout the year, where you can find everything from fresh local produce to handmade crafts and vintage items. These markets offer a chance to experience the city's lively atmosphere while picking up unique items that showcase Brugge's culture.

1. Market Square (Markt)

- **Address**: Markt, 8000 Brugge
- **Phone**: +32 50 44 87 11
- **Website**: www.visitbruges.be

The **Market Square** is the heart of Brugge's shopping scene. On Wednesdays and Saturdays, the square transforms into a bustling market where you can find local vendors selling fresh produce, flowers, artisanal cheeses, meats, and much more.

What to Expect: In addition to food, the market also features street vendors selling handmade goods, vintage items, and souvenirs. It's a great place to wander, sample local treats, and pick up fresh ingredients or a handmade memento from Brugge.

Cost: Prices vary depending on the items, but expect to pay around **€1 to €5** for small items like produce or flowers, with handmade goods priced around **€10 to €30**.

Travel Tip: Visit the market early in the morning for the best selection and quieter crowds. It's a great place to experience the local culture and pick up something special.

2. Brugge Christmas Market

- **Date**: November to January (dates vary)
- **Location**: Market Square, 8000 Brugge
- **Phone**: +32 50 44 87 11
- **Website**: www.christmasinbrugge.be

During the winter season, the **Brugge Christmas Market** transforms the city center into a festive wonderland. Stalls line the streets, selling everything from handmade gifts to delicious Belgian treats, making it a perfect place to shop for unique holiday gifts and souvenirs.

What to Expect: The market offers a variety of local and handmade crafts, including knitted goods, woodwork, and festive ornaments. You'll also find food stalls selling traditional **Belgian waffles**, **frites**, and **mulled wine**, making it a great stop for both shopping and snacking.

Cost: Handmade items range from **€5 to €30**, with larger artisanal gifts priced around **€50+**.

Travel Tip: The market gets quite crowded during weekends, so try to visit on weekdays or early in the day for a more relaxed experience.

3. Sint-Jacobsmarkt (St. Jacob's Market)

- **Address**: Sint-Jacobsstraat, 8000 Brugge
- **Phone**: +32 50 34 87 11

The **Sint-Jacobsmarkt** is a small but charming market that takes place on Sundays. It's a great place to find a mix of second-hand goods, antiques, and collectibles, along with food stalls offering freshly baked bread, local meats, and cheeses.

What to Expect: The market is smaller than the one in Market Square but offers a more relaxed and local atmosphere. It's a good spot to pick up vintage finds, unique collectibles, and traditional Belgian goods.

Cost: Prices for second-hand items and antiques range from **€5 to €50**, depending on the item.

Travel Tip: The market is a hidden gem, not as crowded as other markets, so it's perfect for leisurely browsing and finding one-of-a-kind items.

Where to Find Unique Artisan Goods

Brugge is home to many talented artisans who create high-quality, handmade products. If you're looking for unique, locally crafted goods, here are the best places to shop for something special.

1. Handmade in Brugge

- **Address**: Molenbeekstraat 13, 8000 Brugge
- **Phone**: +32 50 34 21 14

Handmade in Brugge is a store dedicated to showcasing the work of local artisans. It offers a wide variety of handmade goods, from **pottery** and **wooden crafts** to **textiles** and **glassware**. It's the perfect place to pick up a piece of Brugge's artistry.

What to Expect: You'll find a selection of beautifully crafted goods, including pottery, hand-woven textiles, and painted ceramics. The items are both functional and decorative, making them excellent souvenirs or gifts.

Cost: Prices for handmade goods range from **€15 to €80** for smaller items, with larger pieces like pottery vases priced up to **€150**.

Travel Tip: If you're looking for a unique souvenir, a handcrafted ceramic plate or a handwoven scarf from this shop will be a lasting reminder of your visit.

2. Galerie Courtyard

- **Address**: Vlamingstraat 5, 8000 Brugge
- **Phone**: +32 50 34 84 92

For high-quality artisanal jewelry and crafts, **Galerie Courtyard** is a great option. The gallery specializes in handmade **jewelry**, **ceramics**, and **glassworks**, all created by Belgian artists.

What to Expect: The gallery showcases a variety of handmade artisan goods, from delicate silver jewelry to colorful glass sculptures. It's a great place to find something special that reflects the local culture and craftsmanship.

Cost: Jewelry pieces start at **€50**, while larger items like glass sculptures can range from **€80 to €200**.

Travel Tip: The gallery is small but worth a visit if you're looking for a unique gift. Ask the staff about the artists, as they can offer insight into the techniques and stories behind the pieces.

Outdoor Activities and Recreation

Cycling Tours and Rentals in Brugge

Brugge is a city that's perfect for cycling, and it's one of the best ways to explore its charming streets, scenic canals, and surrounding countryside. The city is bike-friendly, with numerous cycling paths that make it easy to explore both the historic center and the quieter areas around Brugge.

Cycling Culture in Brugge

Cycling is a deeply ingrained part of the local culture in Brugge. The city itself is compact and easy to navigate by bike, and the flat terrain makes it accessible for cyclists of all skill levels. You'll see locals riding their bikes daily, whether it's to work, school, or simply for leisure. The city is well-equipped with bike lanes, and cycling is a common mode of transportation for both tourists and residents alike.

Where to Rent Bikes

Brugge has several bike rental shops where visitors can easily rent a bike for a day or longer. Most rental shops offer a variety of bikes, including traditional city bikes, electric bikes, and even tandem bikes. Some of the most well-known bike rental shops include:

(I) Brugge by Bike

- **Address**: Ezelstraat 70, 8000 Brugge
- **Phone**: +32 50 34 94 57
- **Website**: www.bruggebike.be
- **Brugge by Bike** offers a variety of rental bikes, including electric bikes and traditional city bikes. This shop is located close to the city center, making it a convenient choice for tourists looking to explore Brugge on two wheels.
- **Cost**: Bike rentals start at **€10 per day** for a standard bike, with electric bikes priced around **€25 per day**.

(ii) Cycle Bruges

- **Address**: Wijnzakstraat 6, 8000 Brugge
- **Phone**: +32 50 34 38 38
- **Website**: www.cyclebruges.com
- **Cycle Bruges** is another popular choice for bike rentals. They offer a range of bikes including city bikes, mountain bikes, and electric bikes. The shop is conveniently located in the heart of the city, making it easy to pick up your bike and start exploring.
- **Cost**: Rentals for traditional bikes are around **€12 per day**, while electric bikes are priced at **€25 per day**.

Best Cycling Routes in Brugge

Brugge is a flat and bike-friendly city, making it perfect for both leisurely rides and longer cycling tours. Some of the most scenic routes include:

(I) Canal Loop: This is one of the most popular routes, offering views of

Brugge's picturesque canals, historic buildings, and charming streets. The route is easy to follow, and you can stop at various attractions along the way, such as **Minnewater Lake** and the **Belfry Tower**.

(ii) Brugge to Damme Route: This 8-kilometer route takes you from Brugge to the small town of **Damme**, located along the **Oosterstak Canal**. The ride is peaceful, passing through green fields and rural landscapes. Damme itself is home to historic buildings, cafes, and the beautiful **Damme Windmill**.

(iii) Cycling through the Surrounding Countryside: If you're interested in exploring the countryside around Brugge, you can take longer routes that lead to nearby towns and nature reserves. These routes offer a chance to experience the Belgian countryside, with lush fields, windmills, and quaint villages along the way.

Bike Tours

For visitors looking to explore Brugge with a guide, there are several companies offering cycling tours. These guided tours often focus on specific themes, such as Brugge's history, architecture, or local beer culture.

(I) Bike Tour Brugge

- **Website**: www.biketourbrugge.be
- **Bike Tour Brugge** offers a 3-hour guided cycling tour through the city, where you can explore the medieval center, learn about the history of Brugge, and cycle through hidden courtyards and quiet streets. This tour is perfect for those who want to discover Brugge in a more active and informative way.
- **Cost: €25 per person** for a 3-hour guided tour.

(ii) Brugge Cycling Tours

- **Website**: www.bruggecyclingtours.be
- Another great option is **Brugge Cycling Tours**, which offers a range of guided tours including city tours, countryside rides, and specialized tours that focus on local beer or food. The tours are led by knowledgeable guides who share insights into the history and culture of Brugge.
- **Cost**: Prices start at **€20 per person** for a 2-hour city tour.

Walking Tours

Brugge is a city best explored on foot, with its winding streets, hidden courtyards, and stunning medieval architecture.

Self-Guided Walking Tours

If you prefer exploring Brugge at your own pace, a self-guided walking tour is a great option. Brugge is a small city, so most of its attractions are within walking distance of each other. Here are some of the best walking routes you can take to explore the city on foot:

(I) Historic Center Walk: This walking route takes you through Brugge's medieval heart, including landmarks like **Market Square**, the **Belfry Tower**, and the **Basilica of the Holy Blood**. You'll also pass through charming streets like **Ezelstraat** and **Rozenhoedkaai**, where you can enjoy views of the canals and picturesque buildings.

(ii) Brugge's Hidden Courtyards: For a more off-the-beaten-path experience, take a walk through Brugge's hidden courtyards and peaceful alleyways. These tucked-away spots offer a glimpse into the city's past and are perfect for photos. You can find hidden courtyards near **Begijnhof**, **Sint-Janshospitaal**, and along **Katelijnestraat**.

(iii) **Canal Walk**: Brugge is often called the "Venice of the North" because of its beautiful canals. A canal walk is the perfect way to explore the city's waterway system. Start at **Rozenhoedkaai** and follow the canals through the city, stopping at attractions like **Minnewater Park** and the **Swan Lake**.

Organized Walking Tours

If you prefer a guided experience, there are several companies offering walking tours of Brugge. These tours are led by knowledgeable guides who share insights into the city's history, art, and architecture.

(I) Brugge Walks

- **Website**: www.bruggewalks.com
- **Brugge Walks** offers a variety of guided tours, including a general city tour, a **"Brugge in the Middle Ages"** tour, and a **"Brugge's Art and Architecture"** tour. These walking tours provide a deeper understanding of the city's past and present.
- **Cost**: **€15 per person** for a 2-hour guided tour.

(ii) Tourist Information Centre Walking Tours

- **Address**: Markt 14, 8000 Brugge
- **Phone**: +32 50 44 46 46
- The **Tourist Information Centre** offers walking tours led by experienced local guides. The tours are available in several languages and cover a range of topics, including Brugge's history, architecture, and the best places to shop.
- **Cost**: **€10 per person** for a 1.5-hour guided walking tour.

Specialty Walking Tours

For those interested in specific themes, there are also specialty walking tours that focus on different aspects of Brugge's history and culture.

- **Brugge's Beer Walk**: A guided tour that explores Brugge's beer culture, with visits to local breweries and beer shops, and tastings of Belgium's famous brews.
- **Art and Architecture Walk**: A tour that focuses on Brugge's artistic heritage, including its medieval buildings, churches, and art galleries.

Parks and Scenic Views in Brugge

Parks and Green Spaces in Brugge

Brugge is a city known for its historic architecture, but it also has many tranquil parks and green spaces where you can relax, enjoy nature, or have a picnic. If you want a peaceful place to read, watch birds, or simply enjoy the outdoors, Brugge's parks are a perfect escape from the city's bustling streets.

1. Minnewater Park (Lake of Love)

- **Address**: Minnewaterpark, 8000 Brugge
- **Phone**: +32 50 44 87 11

Minnewater Park, also known as the **Lake of Love**, is one of the most picturesque parks in Brugge. It's a peaceful spot that's ideal for a quiet stroll or a relaxing break in nature. The park is famous for its beautiful lake, home to several swans, and its tranquil ambiance, making it a popular spot for both locals and visitors.

What to Expect: The park offers a large, serene lake surrounded by trees, perfect for taking a leisurely walk or sitting on a bench to enjoy the view. The **Minnewater Bridge**, an iconic red-brick bridge, is a great spot for photos. The swans add to the peaceful atmosphere, and it's a wonderful place to enjoy the beauty of Brugge's natural surroundings.

Activities: The park is great for birdwatching, especially in the early morning or late afternoon. It's also a fantastic spot for a picnic with a scenic view of the lake and the swans. For a romantic experience, you can also take a boat ride on the lake, which offers a unique view of the park.

Cost: Free to visit.

Travel Tip: Arrive early in the day or during weekdays for a more peaceful experience. The park can get busier on weekends and holidays.

2. Begijnhof

- **Address**: Wijngaardstraat 19, 8000 Brugge
- **Phone**: +32 50 44 87 11

The **Begijnhof** (Beguine Convent) is a tranquil spot in Brugge that's perfect for a quiet escape. This historical site is home to a beautiful courtyard surrounded by white-washed buildings, where the **Beguines** (a religious order of women) lived in the past. Today, the Begijnhof remains a peaceful retreat for visitors.

What to Expect: The **Begijnhof** is known for its peaceful atmosphere and well-maintained gardens. The **Begijnhof Chapel**, located at the center of the complex, is a beautiful and calming place to visit. The surrounding green space is great for a stroll or a quiet moment of reflection.

Activities: The Begijnhof is a perfect spot for birdwatching, with several species of birds found in the gardens. You can also relax on the benches, take in the peaceful ambiance, and enjoy the stunning white buildings. The Begijnhof is also a great place for families, as it offers a calm, safe environment for children to explore.

Cost: Free to visit the courtyard, but a small donation is suggested for entry to the chapel.

Travel Tip: Visit early in the morning or later in the afternoon to avoid the crowds. The **Begijnhof** is located close to **Minnewater Park**, so you can easily combine a visit to both places in one day.

2. Arentshof

- **Address**: Arentshof, 8000 Brugge
- **Phone**: +32 50 44 87 11

Arentshof is another lovely park in Brugge, located along the canals. This park is less crowded than some of the more popular spots but still offers a peaceful place to relax and enjoy nature. The park has a small pond, green lawns, and several benches perfect for sitting and watching the world go by.

What to Expect: The park is known for its quiet atmosphere and beautiful flowers. It's a great place to take a break from sightseeing, and it's often a favorite spot for locals to relax. The **canal-side** location adds to the park's charm, making it a nice spot for a stroll.

Activities: You can enjoy walking, birdwatching, or simply relaxing on the grass. The park is also home to various plants and flowers, making it a great spot for nature lovers.

Cost: Free to visit.

Travel Tip: If you're looking for a quieter park away from the main tourist attractions, **Arentshof** is a great choice. It's especially peaceful in the mornings.

Scenic Views and Photography Spots

Brugge is a city made for photographers, with its medieval buildings, canals, and charming streets offering countless opportunities for beautiful shots. It doesn't matter you're capturing the stunning views of the canals, the impressive Belfry Tower, or the windmills on the outskirts of town, there are plenty of scenic spots that will give you the perfect picture of Brugge.

1. Belfry Tower

- **Address**: Markt 7, 8000 Brugge
- **Phone**: +32 50 44 46 46
- **Website**: www.belfortbrugge.be

The **Belfry Tower** is one of the most iconic landmarks in Brugge, offering panoramic views of the entire city. Visitors can climb the 366 steps to reach the top and enjoy breathtaking views of the city's rooftops, canals, and nearby countryside.

What to Expect: From the top of the Belfry Tower, you'll have a 360-degree view of Brugge. The view of the **Market Square**, with its historic buildings and the **Belfry**, is particularly stunning. The **canals** and **Minnewater Park** can also be seen from the tower, providing a perfect photography opportunity.

Best Time for Photography: The best times to visit for photos are early in the morning or late afternoon, when the lighting is softer and the crowds are fewer.

Cost: **€12** for adults, **€8** for children 6-12 years old.

Travel Tip: The climb to the top can be strenuous, so wear comfortable shoes. Be sure to bring a camera, as the view is one of the best in the city.

2. Rozenhoedkaai

- **Address**: Rozenhoedkaai, 8000 Brugge
- **Phone**: +32 50 44 87 11

Rozenhoedkaai is one of the most photographed spots in Brugge, offering a beautiful view of the canals, the **historic buildings**, and the **Belfry Tower**. The area is known for its stunning reflections, which make for great photography, especially in the early morning or late evening when the light is perfect.

What to Expect: The view of the canal, with the old buildings and **Minnewater** in the background, is iconic. It's a great spot for photos, particularly during the golden hour when the light reflects beautifully off the water.

Best Time for Photography: The early morning and late evening offer the best light for photography, especially with the reflections in the canal. The area can get busy during the day, so it's best to visit early or late.

Cost: Free to visit.

Travel Tip: This is a great spot for sunset photos, as the light creates stunning colors over the canal and buildings.

3. Windmills on the Outskirts of Brugge

- **Address**: Windmill Road, 8000 Brugge
- **Phone**: +32 50 44 87 11

The windmills on the outskirts of Brugge are a must-see for anyone interested in traditional Belgian architecture and countryside views. These windmills are located just outside the city center, along the **Ringvaart Canal**.

What to Expect: There are several windmills in the area, including the **Sint-Janshuismolen** and **Koeleweimolen**. These windmills offer a great opportunity for photography, with the windmills set against the backdrop of green fields and canals.

Best Time for Photography: Early morning or late afternoon provides the best light for capturing the windmills, especially when the sun casts long shadows and the landscape looks golden.

Cost: Free to visit, but there may be a small fee if you want to enter the windmills.

Travel Tip: The windmills are a bit further from the city center, so consider renting a bike or taking a short bus ride to reach them. The area is peaceful and ideal for a quiet walk or bike ride.

4. Canals of Brugge

- **Address**: Various locations around the city
- **Phone**: +32 50 44 87 11

The canals are the heart of Brugge and offer some of the best views in the city. From **Rozenhoedkaai** to the **Dijver Canal**, there are plenty of scenic spots where you can take stunning photos of the canals, bridges, and medieval buildings.

What to Expect: The canals of Brugge provide countless opportunities for photos, whether you're capturing the reflections of the buildings on the water or the charming boat tours that pass by. The most iconic canal views include **Rozenhoedkaai** and the **Canal Loop**.

Best Time for Photography: The canals are at their most photogenic early in the morning or at sunset, when the light is softer, and the buildings reflect beautifully on the water.

Cost: Free to visit.

Travel Tip: Take a boat tour along the canals for a unique perspective of Brugge, especially if you want to photograph the city from the water.

Water Sports

Water Sports and Canal Activities

Brugge's canals are not only a picturesque backdrop to the city's medieval architecture, but they also offer a variety of water-based activities for visitors seeking adventure or a peaceful way to explore.

1. Paddle Boats and Rowboats

For those looking for a leisurely way to enjoy the canals, renting a **paddle boat** or **rowboat** is a fantastic option. These boats are ideal for families, couples, or anyone who wants to spend time on the water at their own pace.

Where to Rent:

- **Rent a Boat Brugge**
- **Address**: Dijver, 8000 Brugge
- **Phone**: +32 50 34 36 16
- **Website**: www.rentaboatbrugge.be
- This rental service offers a selection of rowboats and paddle boats. The boats can accommodate up to 4 people, making them ideal for a small group or family. Rent a boat and explore the canals at your own pace, taking in Brugge's stunning views as you float down the water.

- **Cost**: Rental prices start at **€15 for an hour** for a small paddle boat, with larger boats available for **€30 for an hour**.
- **Travel Tip**: It's best to book in advance during peak tourist season to secure your boat rental. Consider going early in the morning or late afternoon to avoid crowds and enjoy a quieter experience.
- **What to Expect**: Glide through the quiet canals, enjoying the calm waters and the historic buildings lining the banks. You'll be able to explore the canals of Brugge from a different perspective, passing under bridges and past beautiful old houses. The canals are peaceful, with fewer tourists compared to the traditional boat tours, allowing for a more private and relaxed experience.

2. Kayaking Tours

For those seeking a more active experience, **kayaking** on the canals of Brugge is a great way to enjoy the city's waterways. Kayaks offer a more intimate and agile way to explore the canals, allowing you to venture into quieter areas that are less accessible by larger boats.

Where to Rent Kayaks:

- **Brugge Kayak Tours**
- **Address**: Rozenhoedkaai, 8000 Brugge
- **Phone**: +32 50 34 53 85
- **Website**: www.bruggekayak.be
- **Brugge Kayak Tours** offers guided kayak tours, where you can paddle through the city's canals while learning about Brugge's history. It's an enjoyable and informative way to experience the city on water.
- **Cost**: Kayak rentals are available for around **€20 to €30 per person** for a 1.5-hour guided tour.
- **Travel Tip**: If you're not familiar with kayaking, a guided tour is a great option to ensure you have a safe and enjoyable experience. The tours are

led by knowledgeable guides who provide insight into the history of the canals and Brugge.
- **What to Expect**: During a kayaking tour, you'll paddle through both busy and quieter parts of Brugge. The smaller size of the kayak allows you to navigate the narrower sections of the canals, where traditional boats cannot go. The tours often stop at scenic spots, allowing for photo opportunities and brief pauses to learn more about the landmarks.

3. Private Boat Rentals

If you're looking for a more exclusive and private experience on the canals, renting a private boat is a great option. These boats come with a captain or can be rented without one, depending on your preference. It's the perfect way to enjoy Brugge's waterways without the crowds.

Where to Rent Private Boats:

- **Private Canal Tours Brugge**
- **Address**: Rozenhoedkaai, 8000 Brugge
- **Phone**: +32 50 34 35 70
- **Website**: www.privatecanaltoursbrugge.be
- This company offers private boat rentals, allowing you to explore the canals of Brugge in complete privacy. You can choose to have a private guide or simply enjoy the serenity of the water on your own.
- **Cost**: Prices for private boats start at **€50 per hour** for a small boat and can go up to **€150+ per hour** for larger boats with a guide.
- **Travel Tip**: For a more intimate experience, rent a boat in the evening when the city is quieter, and the canals are beautifully lit by street lamps.
- **What to Expect**: Renting a private boat gives you complete control of your route and pace. You'll have the freedom to explore the canals on your terms, whether you're looking to enjoy the views or just relax in the calm waters. Private boats are ideal for special occasions like romantic

getaways, family gatherings, or simply for those who want a more peaceful experience.

4. Evening Canal Cruises

For a romantic or relaxing way to enjoy the canals, consider booking an **evening canal cruise**. These cruises are typically shorter than daytime tours but offer a unique experience as the sun sets and the city lights reflect off the water.

Where to Book Evening Cruises:

- **Brugge Evening Canal Cruises**
- **Address**: Rozenhoedkaai, 8000 Brugge
- **Phone**: +32 50 34 36 16
- **Website**: www.eveningcanalcruisebrugge.be
- Evening canal cruises offer a peaceful way to see the city's canals, with fewer tourists and a serene atmosphere. As the boat glides along the canals, you'll enjoy the soft evening light and reflections of the city's medieval buildings.
- **Cost**: Evening cruises generally cost around **€20 to €25 per person**.
- **Travel Tip**: Evening cruises are especially charming during the summer months when the weather is mild. Be sure to bring a jacket if you plan to go on a cruise during cooler months.
- **What to Expect**: These evening cruises provide a relaxed and intimate experience. As you glide through the canals, you'll get to see Brugge from a different perspective. The quiet, reflective waters and illuminated buildings create a romantic atmosphere, making this activity perfect for couples or anyone wanting to enjoy a peaceful moment in Brugge.

5. Water-Based Activities for Families

WATER SPORTS

Brugge is also an excellent destination for families looking for water-based activities. Paddle boats and rowboats are ideal for families, as they allow everyone to get involved and explore together. Some companies offer family-friendly boat tours, which provide a more relaxed way to enjoy the canals while learning about Brugge's history.

- **Family-Friendly Boat Rentals**:
- **Rent a Boat Brugge** also offers **family-sized boats**, where parents and children can enjoy a relaxed ride along the canals.
- **Cost**: Family-friendly paddle boats start at **€15 per hour**, making them an affordable option for families.
- **What to Expect**: Families can enjoy the canals from the comfort of a boat, taking in the views, watching for birds, and making memories as they glide through the waterways. The canals provide a calm, safe environment, perfect for children.

Day Trips from Brugge

Ghent

Ghent, often overshadowed by its more famous neighbor Brugge, is a city full of history, culture, and charm. A day trip to Ghent offers visitors the chance to explore one of Belgium's most vibrant cities, with its stunning medieval architecture, world-class museums, and lively atmosphere. Whether you're into history, art, or simply enjoying the city's canals, Ghent has something for everyone.

Must-See Attractions in Ghent

1. Gravensteen Castle

- **Address**: Gravensteen 1, 9000 Gent
- **Phone**: +32 9 222 41 40
- **Website**: www.gravensteen.be

The **Gravensteen Castle**, or **Castle of the Counts**, is one of Ghent's most iconic landmarks. This medieval fortress, originally built in the 12th century, offers a fascinating look into the city's past. Visitors can explore the castle's towers, walls, and the museum inside, which tells the story of Ghent's medieval history and the lives of the counts who ruled here.

What to Expect: You'll walk through rooms filled with medieval weapons, armory, and exhibits on the history of the castle. From the top of the castle, you get a panoramic view of Ghent, which is perfect for photos.

Cost: €10 for adults, €5 for children (6-18 years old).

Travel Tip: Arrive early to avoid crowds, especially on weekends. The castle is centrally located, so it's easy to combine with other nearby attractions.

2. St. Bavo's Cathedral

- **Address**: Sint-Baafsplein, 9000 Ghent
- **Phone**: +32 9 225 39 26
- **Website**: www.sintbaafskathedraal.be

St. Bavo's Cathedral is a must-visit for art lovers and history buffs. This stunning Gothic cathedral is home to the famous **Ghent Altarpiece** by the Van Eyck brothers, one of the most celebrated works of art in the world.

What to Expect: The cathedral's impressive interior features stunning stained glass windows, intricate carvings, and the famous **Adoration of the Mystic Lamb** altarpiece. You can also climb the tower for a beautiful view of the city.

Cost: €4 for general entry. The altarpiece viewing is included in the ticket price, but there may be additional fees for tower access.

Travel Tip: The cathedral can get crowded, especially with tourists visiting the altarpiece. Consider visiting early in the morning to avoid the crowds.

3. Museum of Fine Arts (MSK)

- **Address**: Jan Breydelstraat 5, 9000 Ghent
- **Phone**: +32 9 267 90 50
- **Website**: www.mskgent.be

If you're an art lover, the **Museum of Fine Arts** in Ghent is a top stop. The museum houses a significant collection of works from the Middle Ages to the 20th century, including pieces by Flemish Masters like **Van Eyck**, **Rubens**, and **Memling**.

What to Expect: The collection spans centuries of Flemish and European art, with highlights from the **Renaissance**, **Baroque**, and **Modern periods**. The museum's setting is peaceful, offering a quiet space to explore the world of art.

Cost: €10 for adults, free for children under 18.

Travel Tip: Combine your visit to the Museum of Fine Arts with a stroll through the **Citadelpark**, located nearby. The park is a beautiful, green area perfect for relaxing.

Getting to Ghent from Brugge

Getting to Ghent from Brugge is easy and convenient, with multiple transportation options available.

- **By Train**: The train is the fastest and most convenient way to travel from Brugge to Ghent. Trains run frequently throughout the day from **Brugge Station** to **Ghent St. Pieters Station**, with a journey time of around **30 minutes**.
- **Cost**: Tickets typically cost around **€9-€12** for a one-way trip.
- **Travel Tip**: Check the train schedules ahead of time to plan your trip. You can find timetables and buy tickets at the station or online through the **SNCB** website.

- **By Car**: If you prefer to drive, the distance between Brugge and Ghent is about **50 kilometers** (31 miles), and it takes roughly **40 minutes** by car. The most direct route is via the **E40 motorway**.
- **Cost**: If renting a car, expect prices starting from **€30-€50 per day** depending on the rental agency and vehicle type.
- **Travel Tip**: Parking in Ghent can be difficult, especially in the city center. It's better to park at a **Park and Ride** facility and take public transport into the heart of the city.

Making the Most of Your Day in Ghent

To make the most of your day trip, start with the **Gravensteen Castle** early in the day, followed by **St. Bavo's Cathedral** for a deeper dive into the city's history and art. After lunch, visit the **Museum of Fine Arts** and explore the beautiful **Citadelpark**. You can wrap up your visit by walking along the **Korenmarkt** and enjoying the lively atmosphere of the city's main square.

The Coastline

For a change of pace from Brugge's medieval charm, a day trip to the Belgian coast offers a perfect opportunity to relax by the sea. Whether you prefer the bustling beach town of **Oostende** or the quieter seaside village of **Zeebrugge**, the Belgian coast is just a short distance from Brugge and offers plenty of opportunities for swimming, strolling along the pier, or enjoying fresh seafood.

1. Oostende

- **Address**: Oostende, Belgium

- **Phone**: +32 59 70 11 11
- **Website**: www.oostende.be

Oostende is one of Belgium's most popular beach destinations, known for its wide sandy beaches, lively promenade, and vibrant cultural scene. Located along the North Sea, Oostende has been a favorite seaside getaway for Belgians for decades.

What to Expect: The city offers a long stretch of beach perfect for swimming, sunbathing, or just relaxing with a view of the North Sea. The **Oostende Pier** is an iconic spot for a scenic walk and photo opportunities. The town also has a bustling **seafront promenade** lined with restaurants, cafes, and shops.

Things to Do:

- **Visit the Oostende Pier**: A walk along the pier offers stunning views of the sea, especially at sunset.
- **Swim or Sunbathe**: The beach is perfect for a relaxing day, with plenty of space to spread out.
- **Explore the Ostend Museum**: If you're interested in culture, head to the **Mu.ZEE** museum, which showcases Belgian art from the 19th and 20th centuries.
- **Cost**: The beach is free, but some attractions, such as museums or parking, may charge a fee. Expect to pay around €2-€5 for museum entry.
- **Getting There**: From Brugge, you can take a direct train to **Oostende Station**, which takes about **30 minutes**.
- **Cost**: A one-way ticket costs around €6-€10.

2. Zeebrugge

- **Address**: Zeebrugge, Belgium
- **Phone**: +32 50 55 10 72

- **Website**: www.zeebrugge.be

Zeebrugge, a small coastal village near Brugge, offers a more relaxed, quieter beach experience compared to Oostende. Known for its long, sandy beaches and fishing port, Zeebrugge is a perfect destination for those seeking a peaceful day by the sea.

What to Expect: Zeebrugge's beach is wide and clean, making it ideal for walking, swimming, or simply relaxing. The village also has a small promenade with local shops and cafes where you can enjoy freshly caught seafood.

Things to Do:

- **Walk the Zeebrugge Pier**: This pier offers beautiful views of the coast and is perfect for a leisurely walk.
- **Visit the Seafront**: If you're into seafood, Zeebrugge is home to a great selection of seafood restaurants where you can try the catch of the day.
- **Cost**: The beach is free to visit. Restaurants and cafes typically charge €10-€30 for a meal, depending on where you go.
- **Getting There**: Zeebrugge is only about a **20-minute drive** from Brugge. Alternatively, take a **train to Zeebrugge-Dorp** and then a short bus ride to the beach.
- **Cost**: Train tickets are around €3-€5, and the bus fare is about €2.

Tips for the Beach

- **Best Time to Visit**: The summer months, from June to September, are the best time for a day at the beach, with warmer temperatures and clear skies. If you're visiting in the off-season, be prepared for cooler temperatures and less crowded beaches.

- **What to Bring**: Don't forget sunscreen, a hat, and comfortable shoes for walking along the beach and the pier.

Brussels and The Flemish Countryside

A Day in the Capital

Brussels, Belgium's bustling capital, is just an hour's train ride from Brugge, making it an ideal day trip destination. The city is a vibrant blend of historic landmarks, modern architecture, and international influence. From medieval squares to iconic modernist structures, there's much to see and do in this dynamic city.

Must-See Attractions in Brussels

1. Grand Place

- **Address**: Grand Place, 1000 Brussels
- **Phone**: +32 2 279 43 14
- **Website**: www.grandplace.be

The **Grand Place** is Brussels' historic heart and one of the most beautiful squares in Europe. Surrounded by ornate guildhalls, the **Town Hall**, and **King's House**, this UNESCO World Heritage site is the perfect starting point for your Brussels adventure.

What to Expect: The Grand Place is particularly stunning at night when the buildings are lit up, creating a magical atmosphere. The square is also home to various events throughout the year, such as flower carpets in August and a light show in December.

Cost: Free to visit the square; however, entry to the **Town Hall** or **Museum of the City of Brussels** costs about **€8**.

Travel Tip: The Grand Place can get crowded, especially during peak tourist seasons. Visit early in the morning or later in the evening for a quieter experience.

2. Atomium

- **Address**: Square de l'Atomium, 1020 Brussels
- **Phone**: +32 2 475 47 75
- **Website**: www.atomium.be

The **Atomium** is Brussels' most famous landmark and an architectural wonder. Built for the 1958 World Expo, it's a giant replica of an iron crystal, standing at 102 meters tall. It offers fantastic views of the city and fascinating exhibitions inside its spheres.

What to Expect: The Atomium has nine spheres connected by tubes, and visitors can take an elevator to the top sphere for panoramic views. Inside, you'll find exhibitions on science, design, and Brussels' history. The futuristic design of the structure itself is a photographer's dream.

Cost: **€16** for adults, **€8** for children (6-18 years old).

Travel Tip: If you have time, also visit the nearby **Bruparck**, an entertainment area that includes **Mini-Europe**, a miniature park featuring replicas of European landmarks.

3. Manneken Pis

- **Address**: Rue de l'Étuve 46, 1000 Brussels
- **Phone**: +32 2 513 47 55
- **Website**: www.mannekenpis.brussels

Manneken Pis is a small, bronze statue of a boy peeing into a fountain, located just a few minutes' walk from the Grand Place. Though it's one of the world's smallest landmarks, it's a must-see for visitors to Brussels, often regarded as a symbol of the city's irreverent sense of humor.

What to Expect: The statue is dressed in various costumes throughout the year, and you might catch it in one of its many outfits during your visit. It's a quirky, fun spot to take a quick photo.

Cost: Free.

Travel Tip: Manneken Pis can be surrounded by crowds, so try to visit early in the morning or later in the evening when it's less busy.

Getting to Brussels from Brugge

The easiest way to get from Brugge to Brussels is by train. Trains run frequently from **Brugge Station** to **Brussels Central Station**, with the journey taking about **1 hour**.

- **Cost**: A one-way ticket typically costs between **€9 to €12**.
- **Travel Tip**: Check the train schedules ahead of time at the **SNCB** website or at the station. Trains to Brussels are frequent, but traveling during peak hours may mean a crowded ride.

For those who prefer to drive, it's about **100 kilometers** from Brugge to Brussels, which takes around **1 hour and 15 minutes**. The easiest route is via the **E40 motorway**.

Peaceful Getaways

The Flemish countryside offers a welcome escape from the bustling city life. From charming towns to scenic bike rides and hikes, it's the perfect destination for those who want to unwind and experience the rural beauty of Belgium.

1. Damme

- **Address**: Damme, 8340 West Flanders, Belgium
- **Phone**: +32 50 28 88 10
- **Website**: www.damme.be

Just a short distance from Brugge, the charming town of **Damme** is an ideal day trip. With its quiet canals, medieval architecture, and scenic surroundings, it's a peaceful escape from the city. The town is also known for its **booksellers** and **antique shops**, making it a lovely spot for strolling and browsing.

What to Expect: The town is home to beautiful **canals**, **old windmills**, and picturesque streets lined with historic buildings. Don't miss the **Damme Windmill**, a restored 18th-century mill that provides a great photo opportunity.

- **Things to Do**:
- **Walk or cycle along the canal**: The town is perfect for a leisurely walk or bike ride, with scenic views along the water and plenty of quaint spots to relax.
- **Visit the Damme Church**: The **St. John the Baptist Church** is a beautiful example of **Gothic architecture**, and it's worth a visit while exploring the

town.
- **Cost**: Free to wander the town; the **Damme Windmill** entry is typically around **€3**.
- **Getting There**: You can take a short **15-minute bus ride** or bike from Brugge to Damme. Alternatively, if you enjoy cycling, there are bike routes that lead directly to Damme from Brugge.

2. Windmills of the Flemish Countryside

- **Location**: Various locations near Brugge, such as **Sint-Janshuismolen** and **Koeleweimolen**

The **windmills** of the Flemish countryside are a must-see for anyone wanting to experience the charm of rural Belgium. The area around Brugge is dotted with traditional **windmills**, many of which have been carefully preserved and are still in working condition.

What to Expect: The **windmills** in the surrounding countryside, like those near **Damme**, are perfect for a scenic bike ride or hike. The windmills are often located in peaceful, open spaces with views of the surrounding fields and waterways.

- **Things to Do**:
- **Explore by bike**: There are bike paths that take you past some of the best-preserved windmills in Belgium. Cycling is a great way to enjoy the fresh air and the beautiful countryside.
- **Learn about windmill history**: Many of the windmills have informative plaques explaining their history and how they were used to grind grain or pump water.
- **Cost**: Free to visit the windmills; however, some may charge a small fee for entry if you wish to go inside and see the mechanisms in action.
- **Getting There**: These windmills are easily accessible by bike from Brugge,

with routes that pass through scenic farmland and quaint villages. You can also rent bikes in Brugge and cycle to the windmills as part of a guided tour.

3. Scenic Hikes and Bike Paths

For those looking for a more active day in the countryside, the Flemish countryside offers numerous **hiking** and **bike paths** that allow visitors to experience the rural beauty up close.

- **Hiking Trails in the Countryside**: There are several **hiking routes** around Brugge and in the surrounding villages. You can walk through the peaceful **polder landscapes**, alongside canals, and through small villages like **Damme** or **Lissewege**.
- **Bike Paths**: The area is known for its extensive network of **bike paths**, including routes along the canals, through the countryside, and to nearby towns like **Oostkamp** and **Beernem**.
- **Cost**: Free to hike or bike, though bike rentals generally cost around **€12-€20 per day**.

Local Farms and Belgian Produce

For a taste of rural Belgium, consider visiting one of the **local farms** in the area. Many farms offer tours where you can learn about farming practices and taste fresh local produce.

Farm Visits: Several farms in the area around Brugge offer tours and have onsite shops where you can buy fresh produce, cheeses, and other local products.

Cost: Farm visits are often free, though some may charge a small fee for guided tours or product tasting sessions.

Getting There: Local farms are often accessible by bike or short drives from Brugge. Many bike rental shops can provide maps with routes to local farms.

Itineraries for Every Type of Traveler

One Day in Brugge

Brugge is a small, compact city, making it perfect for a quick yet fulfilling day trip. If you're short on time and want to make the most of your day, here's a one-day itinerary that covers the must-see highlights of Brugge. This itinerary includes iconic sights, scenic walking routes, and a canal boat tour to give you the full Brugge experience in just one day.

Morning: Start with Market Square and Belfry Tower

- **Start Time**: 9:00 AM
- **Duration**: 1 hour

Begin your day at **Market Square (Markt)**, the heart of Brugge. This large, cobbled square is surrounded by stunning medieval buildings, including the **Belfry Tower**, the **Town Hall**, and the **House of the Dukes of Burgundy**. Spend some time admiring the architecture and soaking in the atmosphere of this historic square.

Market Square: The square is home to colorful guildhalls and historic buildings. You'll immediately be struck by the beauty of the area. If you're visiting in the morning, there may be fewer crowds, giving you a more peaceful experience.

Belfry Tower: The Belfry is a must-see in Brugge. Standing tall above the square, the tower offers a 360-degree view of the city. You can climb the **366 steps** to reach the top for panoramic views. Plan to spend about 30 minutes here.

- **Cost**:
- **Market Square**: Free
- **Belfry Tower**: €12 for adults, €8 for children (6-12 years old)
- **Address**: Market Square, 8000 Brugge
- **Phone**: +32 50 44 46 46

Mid-Morning: Canal Boat Tour

- **Time**: 10:30 AM – 11:30 AM
- **Duration**: 1 hour

After visiting the Belfry Tower, take a canal boat tour to explore Brugge from the water. The canals are one of the most iconic features of the city, offering picturesque views of medieval buildings, bridges, and serene waters.

Canal Boat Tour: The boat tours last about **45 minutes** to 1 hour and take you along the canals, passing under charming bridges and past beautiful old buildings. This is one of the best ways to see the city, as you get to view Brugge from a different angle.

- **Cost**:
- Boat tours typically cost around **€10 to €12 per person**.
- **Location**: Depart from **Rozenhoedkaai** or **Dijver**

- **Phone**: +32 50 34 36 16

Lunch Break: Local Café

- **Time**: 12:00 PM – 1:00 PM
- **Duration**: 1 hour

After your canal boat tour, take a break at a local café for lunch. Brugge is known for its delicious **Belgian waffles**, **frites**, and **chocolates**. Find a café along the canal or in one of the quiet squares for a relaxing meal.

Recommendations: Look for a café near **Burg Square** or **Market Square** for easy access to the next attractions.

Afternoon: Visit the Basilica of the Holy Blood and Begijnhof

- **Time**: 1:30 PM – 3:00 PM
- **Duration**: 1.5 hours

After lunch, head to the **Basilica of the Holy Blood**, a beautiful church that houses a relic believed to be the blood of Christ. The basilica is located near **Burg Square**, so it's just a short walk away from the Market Square. Spend some time exploring the church and its surroundings.

Basilica of the Holy Blood: The basilica is one of Brugge's most important religious sites. The architecture is stunning, and it's worth taking the time to visit. Don't forget to check out the **Treasury** for some additional history on the relic.

Begijnhof: After visiting the basilica, take a short walk to the **Begijnhof** (Beguine Convent). This peaceful, hidden courtyard offers a quiet escape from the city's hustle and bustle. It's a great spot for a leisurely stroll and to admire the **Gothic architecture**.

- **Cost**:
- **Basilica of the Holy Blood**: Free, donations are welcome
- **Begijnhof**: Free
- **Address**: Begijnhof 3, 8000 Brugge
- **Phone**: +32 50 44 87 11

Late Afternoon: Visit the Chocolate Museum

- **Time**: 3:30 PM – 4:30 PM
- **Duration**: 1 hour

No trip to Brugge is complete without experiencing its famous chocolate. Head to the **Choco-Story Museum** to learn about the history of chocolate and Belgium's famous chocolate-making tradition. The museum is interactive and fun for all ages, and you'll have the chance to sample some chocolate at the end.

- **Cost**:
- €10 for adults, €7 for children
- **Address**: Wijnzakstraat 2, 8000 Brugge
- **Phone**: +32 50 34 12 43

End of Day: Relax by Minnewater Park

- **Time**: 5:00 PM – 6:00 PM
- **Duration**: 1 hour

Finish your day with a relaxing walk around **Minnewater Park** (Lake of Love), a serene park located just a short walk from the city center. The park is perfect for winding down after a busy day of sightseeing. Enjoy the peaceful surroundings, beautiful swans on the lake, and the charming views of the **Minnewater Bridge**.

- **Cost**: Free
- **Address**: Minnewaterpark, 8000 Brugge
- **Phone**: +32 50 44 87 11

A Romantic Weekend

Brugge is one of Europe's most romantic cities, making it the perfect destination for a romantic weekend getaway. With its charming canals, medieval architecture, and cozy atmosphere, Brugge offers couples a chance to unwind, enjoy intimate experiences, and explore the city at a leisurely pace.

Day 1: Romantic Strolls and Canal Cruises

Start your romantic weekend by exploring Brugge's beautiful canals. Take a **private boat tour** to experience the city from the water, where you'll glide past ancient buildings, under romantic bridges, and along quiet canals. A private boat tour adds a personal touch and creates a relaxing atmosphere for you and your partner to enjoy.

- **Private Boat Tour**: Rent a private boat for around **€50 to €100 per hour**, depending on the boat size and length of the tour.
- **Address**: Rozenhoedkaai, 8000 Brugge
- **Phone**: +32 50 34 35 70

After your boat tour, wander through the charming streets of Brugge. Walk hand-in-hand through **Burg Square**, admiring the stunning architecture, and head to **Minnewater Park** for a quiet, romantic stroll around the lake. The peaceful surroundings and beautiful swans make this a perfect spot for a couple's escape.

Evening: Candlelit Dinner and Sunset Views

For a romantic evening, enjoy a **candlelit dinner** at one of Brugge's intimate restaurants. Choose a restaurant that offers a cozy, private atmosphere with views of the canals or the historic town center.

Tip: Many restaurants along the canals offer outdoor seating with beautiful views, perfect for a romantic sunset dinner.

After dinner, take a walk to the **Belfry Tower** for stunning sunset views over the city. The soft evening light, along with Brugge's medieval buildings, creates a magical atmosphere perfect for couples.

Day 2: Explore Hidden Gems and Enjoy Local Treats

On the second day, explore the quieter, less touristy areas of Brugge. Head to **Begijnhof**, a tranquil, secluded courtyard, where you can enjoy the peaceful surroundings and admire the historical architecture.

- **Cost**: Free
- **Address**: Begijnhof 3, 8000 Brugge
- **Phone**: +32 50 44 87 11

In the afternoon, indulge in some **Belgian chocolate** at the **Choco-Story Museum**, where you can sample the finest chocolate while learning about Brugge's chocolate-making history. Take home some chocolates to remember your trip.

- **Cost**: €10 for adults, €7 for children
- **Address**: Wijnzakstraat 2, 8000 Brugge
- **Phone**: +32 50 34 12 43

End your day with a peaceful walk along the **canals**, perhaps stopping for a drink at a cozy café along the way, before returning to your romantic hotel for a relaxing evening.

Brugge with Kids and Cultural Exploration

A Family-Friendly Adventure

B
rugge is a fantastic destination for families with children. The city offers a variety of kid-friendly activities that will keep both the little ones and adults entertained. Here's an itinerary that will help you make the most of your time in the city.

Day 1: Morning – Canal Boat Tour and Market Square

Start your day with a **canal boat tour**. This is one of the most enjoyable ways to experience Brugge's scenic canals while relaxing. Kids will love seeing the city from the water as they pass under picturesque bridges and glide past medieval buildings. Most tours last around **45 minutes** to 1 hour, so it's perfect for younger children with short attention spans.

- **Where to Take the Boat Tour**: Most canal boat tours depart from **Rozenhoedkaai** or **Dijver**. Look for the colorful boats along the canal.
- **Cost**: Around **€10 per adult, €6 for children** (3-12 years old).
- **Travel Tip**: The tours run frequently, but it's a good idea to book tickets in advance, especially during peak seasons.

After the boat tour, head to **Market Square (Markt)**, which is just a short walk from the canal docks. Here, you can let the kids run around and explore. The square is surrounded by beautiful medieval buildings, and it's a great spot for photos. You'll also find **horse-drawn carriage rides** here, which is a fun way for kids to experience the city.

- **Cost**: **Free to visit** Market Square; carriage rides are around **€40 for a 30-minute tour**.
- **Address**: Market Square, 8000 Brugge

Day 1: Afternoon – The Chocolate Museum and Lunch

Next, head to the **Choco-Story Museum**, a family-friendly destination where both kids and adults can learn about Belgium's famous chocolate-making process. The museum is interactive, with displays about the history of chocolate and fun activities like chocolate-making demonstrations.

- **Cost**: **€10 per adult, €7 for children (6-12 years old)**.
- **Address**: Wijnzakstraat 2, 8000 Brugge
- **Phone**: +32 50 34 12 43

After your visit to the museum, enjoy a family-friendly lunch at a nearby café or restaurant. Many places around **Market Square** offer casual dining options with kid-friendly menus, including pasta, sandwiches, and Belgian waffles.

Day 1: Late Afternoon – Visit to Minnewater Park

In the afternoon, take a stroll to **Minnewater Park (Lake of Love)**, which is perfect for families. The park has a large, calm lake where you can see swans and other wildlife, making it an excellent spot for a leisurely walk. The children can enjoy the open space and perhaps even a picnic by the water.

- **Cost**: Free to visit the park.

- **Address**: Minnewaterpark, 8000 Brugge
- **Phone**: +32 50 44 87 11

Evening – Kid-Friendly Dining and Family Accommodations

For dinner, choose a family-friendly restaurant that offers relaxed dining and kid-friendly portions. Brugge has several great spots for casual dining with children, such as places offering **Belgian fries**, **pasta dishes**, and **steaks**. After dinner, head back to your accommodation for a comfortable night's rest.

For family-friendly accommodations, look for places that offer amenities like cribs, kid's meals, and family rooms. Some good options include:

Family-Friendly Hotels in Brugge:

- **Hotel de Orangerie**: This family-friendly hotel is located close to the city center and offers family suites and kid-friendly services.
- **Hotel Ter Brughe**: A great option for families, offering spacious rooms and easy access to major attractions.

A Cultural Exploration of Brugge's Art and History

Brugge is a city rich in history and culture, making it the perfect destination for history and art buffs. The city's well-preserved medieval buildings, museums, and galleries provide a fascinating insight into its past. For a cultural immersion, here's a detailed itinerary focused on Brugge's art and history.

Day 1: Morning – The Belfry Tower and Historical Walking Tour

Start your cultural exploration with a visit to the **Belfry Tower**, one of Brugge's most iconic landmarks. The **Belfry Tower** offers sweeping views of the city, and climbing its **366 steps** provides an excellent vantage point to understand the layout of the medieval city.

- **Cost**: €12 for adults, €8 for children (6-12 years old).
- **Address**: Markt 7, 8000 Brugge
- **Phone**: +32 50 44 46 46

After visiting the Belfry, take a **guided walking tour** of Brugge's historical center. Walking tours provide a deeper understanding of the city's architecture, art, and history. You'll learn about Brugge's role as a major trading hub in the Middle Ages and explore historical streets, squares, and hidden gems.

- **Cost**: Guided tours start around **€15-€20** per person.
- **Duration**: Around **2 hours**.
- **Contact**: You can book tours through local tourist offices or websites like **Brugge Walks** (www.bruggewalks.com).

Day 1: Afternoon – Museums and Art Galleries

After lunch, head to some of Brugge's top museums. The **Groeningemuseum**, located near the city center, showcases an impressive collection of Flemish art, including works by **Jan van Eyck**, **Hans Memling**, and other renowned artists. The museum is small, allowing you to take in the collection at a leisurely pace.

- **Cost**: €12 for adults, €8 for students and seniors.
- **Address**: Dijver 12, 8000 Brugge
- **Phone**: +32 50 44 87 11
- **Website**: www.museabrugge.be

Next, visit the **Memling Museum**, which is housed in the **Sint-Janshospitaal** (Saint John's Hospital), one of the oldest preserved hospital complexes in

Europe. The museum is dedicated to the works of **Hans Memling**, one of the most important Flemish painters of the 15th century.

- **Cost**: €10 for adults, €5 for children (6-18 years old).
- **Address**: Sint-Jansplein 19, 8000 Brugge
- **Phone**: +32 50 44 87 44
- **Website**: www.museabrugge.be

Day 1: Late Afternoon – The Basilica of the Holy Blood and Burg Square

In the late afternoon, make your way to **Burg Square**, a historical heart of Brugge, where you'll find the **Basilica of the Holy Blood**. The basilica is home to the relic believed to contain the blood of Christ. The church's beautiful **Romanesque architecture** and **Gothic additions** make it a must-visit for history and architecture enthusiasts.

- **Cost**: Free entry, donations are welcome.
- **Address**: Burg 13, 8000 Brugge
- **Phone**: +32 50 44 87 11

After visiting the basilica, take some time to admire the **Burg Square**, which is surrounded by stunning medieval buildings like the **City Hall** and the **Old Court of Justice**. The square is a great place to reflect on the day's experiences and enjoy the historical ambiance of Brugge.

- **Cost**: Free to visit the square.
- **Address**: Burg Square, 8000 Brugge

Evening – Explore the City's Historical Streets

Finish your day with a relaxing walk through some of Brugge's historical streets. Wander down **Ezelstraat**, a charming, quiet street that showcases Brugge's old-world charm, or explore **Rozenhoedkaai**, one of the most photographed areas of the city due to its beautiful canal views.

- **Cost**: Free to walk the streets.
- **Address**: Various locations around the city.

Food Lover's Weekend and Scenic Escape

A Food Lover's Weekend

Brugge, with its rich culinary heritage, is a paradise for food lovers. From classic Belgian dishes to indulgent chocolates and beers, the city offers a delectable journey for all your senses. Here's a weekend itinerary for those looking to savor the best of Brugge's food scene.

Day 1: Morning – Start with a Belgian Breakfast and Explore Local Markets

Start your food lover's weekend with a traditional Belgian breakfast. A typical Belgian breakfast often includes fresh bread, butter, jam, cheese, and cold cuts, along with a coffee or hot chocolate.

Where to Eat: **Chez Albert** is known for its delicious **Belgian waffles**, a breakfast treat you can't miss. Located near **Market Square**, it serves freshly made waffles topped with your choice of whipped cream, chocolate, or fresh fruit.

- **Cost**: €5-€10 for waffles.
- **Address**: Vlamingstraat 45, 8000 Brugge
- **Phone**: +32 50 34 93 50

After breakfast, head to **The Markt** for a casual stroll through the square and a visit to the local market (on Wednesdays and Saturdays). It's a great spot for fresh produce, cheeses, meats, and other local delicacies. Many vendors offer samples, so it's a good chance to try local specialties.

- **Cost**: Free to visit the market; however, food items will vary in price based on what you purchase.

Day 1: Mid-Morning – Visit a Chocolate Shop and Try Belgian Truffles

No food lover's trip to Brugge is complete without indulging in some Belgian chocolate. Brugge is home to many artisan chocolate shops that offer handcrafted, high-quality chocolates. Make sure to stop by **Chocolaterie Dumon**, one of the most famous chocolate shops in Brugge. Their **truffles** and **chocolate pralines** are a must-try.

- **Cost**: Chocolates and truffles start at **€10-€15 per box**.
- **Address**: Eiermarkt 6, 8000 Brugge
- **Phone**: +32 50 34 07 51

While in the area, you can also visit **Choco-Story**, the chocolate museum, where you'll learn about the history of chocolate and the Belgian chocolate-making process. The museum also has tastings and interactive experiences.

- **Cost**: **€10** for adults, **€7** for children (6-12 years old).
- **Address**: Wijnzakstraat 2, 8000 Brugge
- **Phone**: +32 50 34 12 43

Day 1: Lunch – Enjoy Classic Belgian Cuisine at a Local Restaurant

For lunch, experience a traditional Belgian dish like **stoofvlees** (beef stew) served with fries, or try a fresh, local **moules-frites** (mussels with fries).

Where to Eat: **De Halve Maan** is a great spot to try **stoofvlees** or other hearty Belgian dishes. It also has a brewery, so you can enjoy a freshly brewed Belgian beer with your meal.

- **Cost**: A main dish ranges from €15 to €20.
- **Address**: Walplein 26, 8000 Brugge
- **Phone**: +32 50 44 41 08

After lunch, take a short walk around the **Burg Square** to digest and enjoy Brugge's historic buildings.

Day 1: Afternoon – Belgian Beer Tasting Tour

Belgium is famous for its beer, and Brugge offers an excellent range of beer experiences. Take a **beer tasting tour** at **De Halve Maan Brewery**, where you can learn about the brewing process and taste some of Brugge's finest beers.

- **Cost**: Beer tasting tours typically cost around €12-€15 per person.
- **Address**: Walplein 26, 8000 Brugge
- **Phone**: +32 50 44 41 08

Alternatively, if you're more of a beer enthusiast, you could visit the **Bierbrasserie Cambrinus**, known for its extensive selection of Belgian beers. They offer tasting flights, so you can sample a variety of beers and pair them with snacks like local cheeses.

- **Cost**: A beer tasting flight starts at €12.
- **Address**: Philipstockstraat 19, 8000 Brugge
- **Phone**: +32 50 34 04 62

Day 1: Evening – Dinner with a View and Belgian Desserts

For dinner, enjoy some fine Belgian cuisine with a view. **Brasserie Cambrinus** offers a wide selection of Belgian dishes with an excellent beer list. Try the **Belgian rabbit stew** or **waterzooi**, a creamy chicken or fish stew that is a classic of the region.

After dinner, head to **Chez Albert** or **The Chocolate Line** for a sweet dessert treat, such as a rich **chocolate mousse** or **Belgian waffles** topped with strawberries and whipped cream.

- **Cost**: Around **€15 to €25 per person** for dinner.
- **Address**: Philipstockstraat 19, 8000 Brugge (Cambrinus)
- **Phone**: +32 50 34 04 62

A Relaxing, Scenic Brugge Escape

Brugge is also a perfect destination for those looking to unwind. With its peaceful canals, charming streets, and serene parks, the city offers plenty of spots to relax and take in the beauty of your surroundings.

Day 1: Morning – Canal-side Cafes and Scenic Strolls

Start your relaxing day with a slow breakfast at a canal-side café. Brugge has plenty of cozy cafés where you can enjoy a hot coffee or a tea with a **Belgian pastry** like a **cinnamon roll** or **Belgian waffle**.

- **Where to Eat**: **The Olive Tree** is a serene café with canal views, perfect for a peaceful start to the day. Enjoy a coffee and pastry while watching the boats drift by.

- **Cost**: A coffee or tea with a pastry will cost around €5-€10.
- **Address**: Ezelstraat 49, 8000 Brugge
- **Phone**: +32 50 34 35 73

After your breakfast, take a gentle stroll along **Rozenhoedkaai** or the **Dijver Canal**, two of the most scenic spots in Brugge. The calm canals and the reflection of the medieval buildings create a tranquil atmosphere, perfect for a peaceful walk.

- **Cost**: Free to walk along the canals.

Day 1: Late Morning – A Visit to Minnewater Park

Next, head to **Minnewater Park (Lake of Love)**, a peaceful green space that is ideal for relaxation. You can walk around the lake, sit by the water, or even enjoy a quiet picnic. The park is home to beautiful swans and offers plenty of benches where you can sit and take in the views.

- **Cost**: Free
- **Address**: Minnewaterpark, 8000 Brugge
- **Phone**: +32 50 44 87 11

Day 1: Afternoon – A Spa Afternoon at a Local Wellness Center

For the ultimate relaxation, spend your afternoon at a **wellness center** or **spa**. Brugge offers a few high-quality spas where you can enjoy treatments like massages, facials, and saunas.

- **Where to Relax**: **Sanisper Spa** is a luxurious option, offering a range of treatments designed to help you unwind and rejuvenate. You can book a **couple's massage** or indulge in a wellness package.

- **Cost**: Treatments start around **€40-€80** depending on the service.
- **Address**: Langestraat 9, 8000 Brugge
- **Phone**: +32 50 34 09 22

Alternatively, **Thermae Boetfort** is located just outside Brugge and offers a full spa experience with thermal baths and wellness treatments.

Day 1: Evening – Sunset Views and Relaxing Dinner

After your spa session, enjoy a relaxing dinner at one of Brugge's intimate restaurants. Many restaurants near the canals offer evening seating, where you can dine and enjoy the soft evening light reflecting on the water.

- **Where to Eat**: **De Halve Maan** is a great option for a calm and relaxing dinner. The restaurant's outdoor seating area by the canal makes for a perfect dining experience. Pair your meal with a glass of Belgian wine or beer for a full experience.
- **Cost**: **€25 to €40** for a meal.
- **Address**: Walplein 26, 8000 Brugge
- **Phone**: +32 50 44 41 08

After dinner, enjoy a leisurely walk along the canals to end your day on a peaceful note. Brugge's streets are especially charming at night when the buildings are illuminated.

Practical Information for Travelers

Currency and Money

Currency in Brugge

The official currency in Brugge, like the rest of Belgium, is the **Euro** (**€**). Banknotes are available in denominations of **€5, €10, €20, €50, €100, €200, and €500**, while coins come in **€1, €2, and 1, 2, 5, 10, 20, and 50 cent coins**.

Exchanging Currency

While you can exchange foreign currency at banks or exchange offices in Brugge, **ATMs** are the most convenient way to withdraw local currency. Many **ATMs** in Brugge allow you to withdraw **Euros** using an international debit or credit card. ATMs are widely available, especially in tourist areas such as **Market Square**, **Burg Square**, and near the **train station**.

- **Currency Exchange Offices**: There are several currency exchange offices in Brugge, such as **Travelex** at **Brugge Station** or **Global Exchange**, located at major tourist areas.
- **Cost**: Currency exchange rates may include a service fee or slightly higher rates, so it's better to compare before exchanging.

- **Tip**: It's a good idea to carry a small amount of Euros for minor purchases or tips, but for larger amounts, withdrawing directly from an ATM is often more economical.

ATMs

ATMs are widely available in Brugge, and you can find them at **banks**, **train stations**, and **shopping areas**. Many ATMs also offer multilingual services, so withdrawing cash is easy for international travelers. Be mindful of any ATM withdrawal fees your home bank may charge, and check the exchange rate to ensure it's competitive.

Where to Find ATMs:

- **Brugge Station**: Multiple ATMs are located in and around the train station.
- **Market Square (Markt)**: Several ATMs are within walking distance of the square.

Using Credit Cards

Most businesses in Brugge, including restaurants, cafes, and shops, accept **major credit cards** like **Visa**, **MasterCard**, and **American Express**. However, it's always a good idea to check before purchasing, especially in smaller shops or markets. Some places may charge a small fee for credit card transactions, but it's not common. For very small purchases, it's often easier to pay in cash.

Credit Card Tips:

- If you're using a credit card, make sure to inform your bank ahead of time to avoid any blocks on your account.

- Most places accept credit cards, but it's always safe to carry some **cash** in case you visit places that don't accept them.

Tipping Practices in Brugge

Tipping in Brugge is similar to the rest of Belgium. Service charges are often included in the bill, so tipping is not mandatory but appreciated. In restaurants, cafes, and taxis, it's customary to leave a small tip as a gesture of appreciation for good service.

Restaurants and Cafes: If the service charge is included in the bill (often listed as "service compris"), you don't need to tip, but leaving **5-10%** of the bill amount is typical for excellent service. If no service charge is included, a tip of **5-10%** is common.

Taxis: For taxi rides, it's common to round up the fare to the nearest **Euro** or leave **5-10%** of the total fare. For example, if your fare is €15, you might round it up to €16 or leave €1 as a tip.

Hotel Staff: Tipping hotel staff such as bellboys or housekeeping is appreciated but not obligatory. Typically, €1-€2 per service is acceptable.

Local Emergency Numbers and Services

While Brugge is a safe city for tourists, it's important to know what to do and who to contact in case of emergencies.

Emergency Numbers in Belgium

In Belgium, the **emergency number** is the same across all services, and you can dial **112** for any emergency.

- **Emergency Number**: **112** – This works for police, ambulance, and fire services.
- **Response Time**: Emergency services typically respond quickly, with **ambulances** arriving within minutes for urgent cases.

Police

If you need the police for a non-urgent matter, such as reporting a lost passport or wallet, or if you need assistance with minor incidents, you can contact the local police station.

- **Police Station**:
- **Address**: **Brugge Police Station**, Dijver 17, 8000 Brugge
- **Phone**: +32 50 44 88 10
- **Emergency Contact**: In case of an emergency requiring immediate police assistance, dial **112** or **101** (local police).

Ambulance and Medical Emergencies

In the case of a medical emergency, whether it's a serious injury, sudden illness, or accident, **ambulances** in Brugge respond swiftly. Dialing **112** is the quickest way to contact **ambulance services**.

- **Nearest Hospital**:
- **AZ Sint-Jan Hospital**
- **Address**: Bruggesteenweg 4, 8000 Brugge
- **Phone**: +32 50 45 45 11
- **Website**: www.azsintjan.be

This hospital is located on the outskirts of Brugge but is well-equipped for emergencies. It's advised to have your **European Health Insurance Card (EHIC)** or travel insurance with you when visiting a hospital.

- **Non-Urgent Care**: For non-urgent medical care or minor illnesses, **general practitioners** (GPs) in Brugge are available. You can contact them for consultations or advice. Most GPs in Brugge speak English.

Fire Department

In case of a fire or fire-related emergency, you can contact the fire department immediately by dialing **112**.

- **Fire Department**:
- **Address**: **Fire Station Brugge**, Aartshertoginnelaan 47, 8000 Brugge
- **Phone**: +32 50 44 99 99

Embassy or Consular Services

For any legal or documentation-related issues while traveling, knowing where your embassy or consulate is located is important. While Brugge does not have an embassy, it's easy to find consulates in nearby **Brussels**.

- **U.S. Embassy in Brussels**:
- **Address**: Boulevard du Régent 27, 1000 Brussels
- **Phone**: +32 2 811 40 00
- **Website**: https://be.usembassy.gov
- **British Embassy in Brussels**:
- **Address**: Regentlaan 1, 1000 Brussels
- **Phone**: +32 2 287 60 11
- **Website**: https://www.gov.uk/world/belgium
- **Canadian Embassy in Brussels**:

- **Address**: 1 Avenue des Arts, 1210 Brussels
- **Phone**: +32 2 512 39 83
- **Website**: www.canadainternational.gc.ca

Pharmacies in Brugge

If you need medication or advice on over-the-counter treatments, pharmacies are available throughout Brugge. Most **pharmacies** also offer a **24-hour emergency service**, where you can get urgent medical supplies outside regular hours.

- **Pharmacy with 24-Hour Service**:
- **Pharmacy De Zalm**
- **Address**: Ezelstraat 74, 8000 Brugge
- **Phone**: +32 50 33 10 62
- **Website**: www.pharmacie-de-zalm.be
- **Standard Pharmacy Hours**: Most pharmacies in Brugge are open from **9 AM to 6 PM**, Monday to Saturday.

Travel Insurance and Staying Connected

Travel Insurance Tips

Travel insurance is a must for any trip, and Brugge is no exception. While Brugge is a safe and welcoming city, unexpected events can still occur, and having travel insurance ensures that you're covered for various emergencies. Here's why you need it and what it should cover.

Why Travel Insurance is Essential

Travel insurance provides peace of mind, knowing that if things go wrong, you have a safety net. A sudden illness, a flight cancellation, or lost luggage can derail your plans. Travel insurance helps mitigate the financial impact of these unexpected events. For an international trip to Brugge, travel insurance can protect you from medical emergencies, trip interruptions, lost luggage, and more.

What Travel Insurance Should Include

When selecting travel insurance, make sure your plan covers the following key areas:

1. Medical Coverage: Health insurance in your home country might not cover you while traveling abroad, so it's crucial to have **medical coverage** as part of your travel insurance. This ensures you're covered for any unexpected medical treatment, including hospital visits, surgeries, and emergency medical evacuation.

- **What It Covers**: Medical treatments, emergency hospitalization, emergency evacuation back to your home country (if necessary), and repatriation.
- **Cost**: Insurance policies vary based on the provider, but expect to pay between **€30-€80** for a short-term policy covering **medical treatment** during your stay in Brugge.
- **How to Get It**: Many travelers choose insurance plans from well-known companies like **World Nomads**, **Allianz Travel**, or **Travel Guard**. These providers offer comprehensive medical coverage for travelers to Europe.

2. **Lost Luggage and Theft Protection**: Luggage can get delayed, lost, or even stolen, so having insurance for lost baggage or personal items is vital. **Travel insurance** can help reimburse you for your lost belongings, including clothes, electronics, and other valuables, making it easier to recover from this inconvenience.

- **What It Covers**: Compensation for lost, delayed, or stolen luggage; reimbursement for essential items like toiletries and clothing.
- **Cost**: Typically included in most policies, but check the policy limits, as higher-value items may require additional coverage.
- **How to Get It**: Ensure your insurance provider offers a **lost luggage** benefit in your plan.

3. **Trip Cancellation or Interruption**: Life is unpredictable, and sometimes you may need to cancel or interrupt your trip due to unforeseen events, such as illness or a family emergency. Trip cancellation coverage ensures that you're

reimbursed for non-refundable deposits and expenses if you must cut your trip short.

- **What It Covers**: Non-refundable flight tickets, hotel bookings, tours, or activities if you need to cancel or cut your trip short.
- **Cost**: Typically ranges from **€40-€100**, depending on the length of the trip and coverage.
- **How to Get It**: Make sure your insurance plan offers coverage for trip cancellations, especially if you've booked activities in Brugge or have non-refundable reservations.

4. **Personal Liability**: Accidents can happen while traveling, and personal liability coverage protects you if you're responsible for accidental injury or damage to others during your trip. This may not be needed by everyone, but it's helpful for those planning activities like renting bikes or driving.

- **What It Covers**: Injuries to others or damage to property that you cause accidentally.
- **Cost**: Generally included in most travel insurance packages, but check your plan for specifics.
- **How to Get It**: Check with your insurance provider to confirm that personal liability coverage is included.

How to Find the Right Plan for Travelers to Brugge

When selecting travel insurance for Brugge, look for an insurance plan that fits your needs. Here are some tips:

1. **Shop Around**: Compare different travel insurance providers to find the best coverage for your needs and budget. Use comparison websites like **Squaremouth** or **InsureMyTrip** to compare plans side by side.

2. Check Exclusions: Always check for exclusions in the policy. For example, some policies may not cover pre-existing medical conditions or certain types of adventure sports.

3. Read the Fine Print: Understand the policy's coverage limits, especially regarding medical expenses, trip cancellations, and lost luggage. Make sure you're aware of any deductibles and reimbursement processes.

4. Buy Early: It's always better to purchase travel insurance before you leave for your trip, as it often covers unexpected events that happen before your departure (such as trip cancellations).

SIM Cards and Wi-Fi

In today's world, staying connected while traveling is important for navigation, communication, and even finding last-minute recommendations. Brugge offers several ways to stay connected, whether you need a local SIM card for your phone or you're simply looking for reliable Wi-Fi spots.

SIM Cards in Brugge

For a seamless connection while in Brugge, getting a **local SIM card** is often the best option. You can buy SIM cards at the **Brugge train station**, major mobile network stores, or even at some supermarkets. Having a Belgian SIM card gives you access to **local rates** for calls, texts, and data.

Where to Buy a SIM Card:

- **Brugge Train Station**: There are mobile shops within the station, like **Proximus** or **Base**, where you can easily buy a SIM card.
- **Supermarkets**: Many supermarkets, like **Carrefour** or **Colruyt**, sell

prepaid SIM cards at reasonable prices.
- **Cost of SIM Cards**:
- **Prepaid SIM cards** typically cost between **€10-€30**, depending on the amount of data and minutes included.
- Look for plans with data allowances of at least **1GB to 5GB** if you plan to use your phone for maps or social media.
- **Top Mobile Providers**:
- **Proximus**: One of the most popular mobile networks in Belgium, offering **data plans**, **calls**, and **SMS services**.
- **Telenet**: Another provider with **affordable data** and coverage across Belgium.
- **Base**: Known for offering **budget-friendly plans** for tourists.

Once you've purchased your SIM card, insert it into your unlocked phone and activate it by following the instructions provided by the provider. Many providers also offer **online registration**, making it easier for tourists to activate their SIM cards.

Wi-Fi in Brugge

Brugge offers a range of options to stay connected to the internet. Many cafes, restaurants, and public areas provide free Wi-Fi, so you can easily access the web to check your email, update social media, or find the best things to do in the city.

Wi-Fi at Cafes and Restaurants:

- Many cafés in Brugge offer **free Wi-Fi** to customers. Some popular places with reliable Wi-Fi include **The Olive Tree**, **Bakkerij (Bakery)**, and **Café De Refter**. These are great spots to relax and catch up on messages while enjoying a coffee or snack.
- **Cost**: Free, but you may need to make a small purchase to access the Wi-Fi.
- **Public Wi-Fi**:

- **Brugge city center** offers several **public Wi-Fi hotspots**, especially around key tourist areas like **Market Square** and **Burg Square**. You can easily access these networks without the need for a SIM card.
- **Cost**: Free, but keep in mind that the quality may vary depending on location.
- **Hotel Wi-Fi**:
- Most hotels in Brugge offer free **Wi-Fi** for their guests. Be sure to check with the hotel when booking to ensure **high-speed internet** is available. If you need **premium** internet for work or streaming, inquire if there's a paid upgrade option.

Mobile Data and Internet Usage Tips

- **Data Roaming**: If you're bringing your phone from outside of Belgium, make sure to **disable data roaming** on your device to avoid high charges from your home carrier. Consider purchasing a local SIM card or using **Wi-Fi** where available.
- **Apps for Local Navigation**: Use apps like **Google Maps** for navigation around Brugge. You can also download the **Visit Brugge** app, which offers helpful details about the city's sights, activities, and events.
- **Internet Speed**: Belgium offers **fast and reliable mobile data** and Wi-Fi in most areas, but some remote spots may experience slower connections. Always check your data plan to avoid overages.

Accessibility for Disabled Travelers and FAQ

Accessibility for Disabled Travelers

Brugge is a city that welcomes all visitors, and while it is an old city with cobbled streets and medieval buildings, the city has made significant efforts to improve accessibility for disabled travelers.

Wheelchair-Friendly Public Transport

Brugge's **public transport** system is relatively accessible, with **buses** and **trains** offering services for travelers with disabilities.

Buses:

- Brugge's **local buses**, operated by **De Lijn**, are mostly **wheelchair accessible**. They feature ramps and low floors for easier boarding. There are designated spaces for wheelchairs, so traveling by bus is a convenient option.
- **Cost**: A single ticket for a local bus ride in Brugge is around €3, but a **mobility pass** may offer discounted rates.
- **Where to Board**: Buses depart from **Brugge Station** and several stops throughout the city.

Trains:

- The main **Brugge train station** (**Station Brugge**) is also accessible, with ramps, elevators, and designated spaces for wheelchair users. There is assistance available at the station, so it's advisable to contact the station ahead of your arrival for support.
- **Cost**: Train fares in Belgium vary, but travelers with disabilities may receive discounts. You can inquire about the specific rates at the station or on the **SNCB** website.
- **Assistance**: You can request assistance at the **SNCB** helpdesk or book it online via their **mobility services**.

Accessible Attractions in Brugge

Brugge offers several **wheelchair-friendly attractions** and sites that are accessible for disabled visitors.

1. Market Square (Markt):

- This bustling square in the heart of Brugge has paved walkways and is largely **wheelchair accessible**. Most of the main attractions around the square, such as the **Belfry Tower** and **City Hall**, are also wheelchair friendly with ramps and elevators.
- **Cost**: Free to enter the square.

2. Belfry Tower:

- The **Belfry Tower** is an iconic landmark in Brugge, and while the narrow stairs may be difficult for those with limited mobility, visitors with wheelchairs can still enjoy the **Market Square** and surrounding views from below.
- **Cost**: €12 for adults, €8 for children.

ACCESSIBILITY FOR DISABLED TRAVELERS AND FAQ

- **Note**: No elevator to the top, but the area around the tower is accessible.

3. Basilica of the Holy Blood:

- The **Basilica of the Holy Blood** offers **wheelchair access** through its main entrance. This historic church, known for housing a relic believed to contain the blood of Christ, has accessible paths and ramps inside.
- **Cost**: Free entry, but donations are appreciated.

4. Canal Boat Tours:

- Some of the canal boat tours in Brugge provide **wheelchair accessible boats**. The boats have ramps, and the tour staff is typically willing to assist passengers with mobility challenges.
- **Cost**: Around €10 to €12 for adults.
- **Where to Board**: **Rozenhoedkaai** or **Dijver** for boat tours.

5. Museums:

- Many museums in Brugge, such as the **Groeningemuseum** (fine arts museum) and **Choco-Story Museum**, are equipped with ramps and elevators for easy access. You can easily navigate through these museums and enjoy the exhibitions.

6. Begijnhof (Beguinage):

- The **Begijnhof**, a historic site in Brugge, has **wide paths and smooth surfaces**, making it accessible for wheelchair users. The peaceful surroundings offer a perfect spot to relax and enjoy the tranquil environment.
- **Cost**: Free.

Accessible Accommodations

Many hotels in Brugge cater to guests with disabilities, offering rooms and facilities that are accessible for wheelchair users. When booking accommodation, always check for **accessible rooms** or facilities. Some places that provide **accessible rooms** include:

- **Hotel de Orangerie**: This hotel offers accessible rooms and is centrally located, making it easy for wheelchair users to access key attractions.
- **Address**: Kartuizerinnenstraat 10, 8000 Brugge
- **Phone**: +32 50 34 50 35
- **NH Brugge**: Located near the **station**, this hotel has accessible rooms and amenities for guests with mobility challenges.
- **Address**: Boeveriestraat 2, 8000 Brugge
- **Phone**: +32 50 67 09 67

Tips for Disabled Travelers in Brugge

1. **Book in Advance**: It's always a good idea to book your transport and accommodation in advance to ensure that the necessary accommodations for your mobility needs are available.

2. **Use Assistance Services**: When arriving at **Brugge Station**, or any other major station, you can request assistance to navigate the station or get to your accommodation. It's better to notify the station staff ahead of time.

3. **Check Attractions**: Always check with the attraction you plan to visit to ensure it meets your accessibility requirements.

ACCESSIBILITY FOR DISABLED TRAVELERS AND FAQ

Answers to Common Travel Questions

1. What's the best way to get around Brugge?

The best way to get around Brugge is by **walking**. The city is compact, and most major attractions are within walking distance of each other. However, for visitors with mobility challenges, Brugge offers **wheelchair accessible buses** and **canal boat tours**. If you're traveling by train, the **Brugge train station** has accessibility features, including elevators and ramps.

- **Walking**: Brugge's streets are generally pedestrian-friendly, though the cobblestones may pose a challenge. If you're concerned about the cobblestones, you may want to plan your route to stick to smoother paths.
- **Public Transport**: The **bus system** in Brugge is quite good and accessible for people with disabilities.
- **Canal Tours**: Some **canal boats** have ramps for easy access. Ask at the dock before purchasing tickets to ensure the boat is wheelchair accessible.

2. How do I get from the airport to the city center?

If you're flying into **Brussels Airport** (BRU), it's easy to get to Brugge by **train**. The train ride takes about **1 hour** and offers a direct connection from the airport to **Brugge Station**. Trains run regularly, and the station at the airport is fully accessible.

Train from Brussels Airport:

- **Cost**: Around €14 for a one-way ticket.
- **Travel Time: 1 hour**.
- **Where to Board**: Trains leave from the **Brussels Airport Railway Station** (located inside the airport).

If you're arriving at **Oostende Airport**, it's a shorter journey by bus, or you can rent a car.

3. Is Brugge a good destination for a family vacation?

Yes, Brugge is an excellent destination for families. There are plenty of kid-friendly activities, including **canal tours**, **chocolate museums**, and **parks** where children can enjoy running around. Families with young children will appreciate the city's walkability and the abundance of **interactive museums**.

- **Kid-Friendly Attractions**:
- **Choco-Story Museum**: Offers a fun, interactive experience for kids.
- **Canal Boat Tours**: Great for a scenic family outing.

4. What are the best times to visit Brugge?

The best time to visit Brugge is during **spring (April to June)** and **autumn (September to November)** when the weather is mild, and the city is less crowded. **Summer** (July and August) is the peak tourist season, so expect more crowds. **Winter** is quiet, and Brugge looks magical with holiday lights and decorations.

- **Weather**: The weather in Brugge can be unpredictable, so it's a good idea to pack layers and an umbrella, especially in the winter months.

5. Is Brugge safe for tourists?

Yes, Brugge is generally a very **safe** city for tourists. Like any popular tourist destination, it's always a good idea to keep an eye on your belongings in crowded areas. Petty theft can occasionally occur, especially in busy spots like **Market Square**.

- **Travel Tips**:
- Use **hotel safes** for valuables.
- Always be cautious in tourist-heavy areas.

Appendices

List of Local Festivals and Events in 2025

Brugge is known for its vibrant festivals and local events, and 2025 promises to be a year full of cultural celebrations, local traditions, and international festivities. Here's a list of the key events and festivals taking place in Brugge throughout the year.

1. Procession of the Holy Blood

- **Dates**: May 21, 2025
- **Description**: The **Procession of the Holy Blood** is one of Brugge's most famous events. This centuries-old religious procession, held every Ascension Day, features a parade through the city's streets carrying a relic believed to contain the blood of Christ. The procession includes colorful floats, music, and participants dressed in medieval costumes, creating a spectacular spectacle.
- **Where to Attend**: The procession departs from **Burg Square** and winds through the historic city center.

2. Brugge Beer Festival

- **Dates**: February 1-2, 2025

- **Description**: Held annually in the **Brugge Concert Hall**, this event celebrates the Belgian beer culture. It brings together more than 70 Belgian brewers offering tastings of a wide range of local beers, including Trappist beers, IPAs, and lagers. The festival also includes workshops and tastings led by experts, making it a must for beer lovers.
- **Where to Attend**: **Concertgebouw**, 't Zand 34, 8000 Brugge.
- **Cost**: Entrance tickets typically cost **€10-€20**, depending on the day.

3. Brugge Christmas Markets

- **Dates**: November 27 – December 31, 2025
- **Description**: The **Brugge Christmas Markets** transform the historic center into a festive wonderland. You'll find over 150 stalls selling handcrafted goods, Christmas decorations, warm beverages, and delicious treats like Belgian waffles and hot chocolate. The **Grote Markt** and **Simon Stevinplein** are main locations for the markets, with lights, music, and seasonal food creating a magical atmosphere.
- **Where to Attend**: **Grote Markt** and **Simon Stevinplein**.
- **Cost**: Free to visit the markets, but expect to pay for food, drinks, and gifts.

4. Music at the Markt

- **Dates**: July 2025 (Exact Dates TBD)
- **Description**: **Music at the Markt** is a series of outdoor concerts held throughout the summer months. Local and international artists perform on a stage set up in **Market Square**, offering everything from classical music to jazz, pop, and folk. It's a great way to enjoy live performances in a beautiful open-air setting.
- **Where to Attend**: **Market Square (Markt)**, 8000 Brugge.
- **Cost**: Free, though donations are encouraged.

5. Brugge Triennale (Art and Architecture Festival)

- **Dates**: May 2025 – September 2025
- **Description**: The **Brugge Triennale** is an international art and architecture festival held every three years. The 2025 edition will showcase contemporary art installations, sculptures, and architectural designs around the city. This event transforms public spaces into open-air galleries, offering an immersive cultural experience for art lovers.
- **Where to Attend**: Various locations throughout Brugge, including **Burg Square**, **Minnewater Park**, and other prominent public spaces.
- **Cost**: €12-€15 for entrance to select exhibitions.

6. Flanders International Film Festival

- **Dates**: October 2025 (Exact Dates TBD)
- **Description**: The **Flanders International Film Festival** showcases a selection of international and Belgian films. The festival features screenings, filmmaker talks, and special events. The festival's focus is on both contemporary cinema and classic films, offering a cultural touchpoint for film lovers visiting Brugge in the fall.
- **Where to Attend**: **CinemaxX Brugge**, Boudewijn Seapark, 8000 Brugge.
- **Cost**: Typically €8-€12 per ticket for screenings.

Directory of Key Attractions and Services

Brugge is a beautiful, walkable city with many key services and attractions that are easily accessible. Whether you need medical services, tourist information, or just want to know where to visit, this directory will help you find what you need.

Key Attractions in Brugge

APPENDICES

1. Market Square (Markt)

- **Address**: Markt, 8000 Brugge
- **What to See**: This iconic square is surrounded by historic buildings and is home to the **Belfry Tower** and the **City Hall**. It's a great place to begin your exploration of Brugge.

2. Belfry Tower

- **Address**: Markt 7, 8000 Brugge
- **Phone**: +32 50 44 46 46
- **What to See**: Climb the **366 steps** for panoramic views of the city. The Belfry is a symbol of Brugge's medieval heritage.

3. Basilica of the Holy Blood

- **Address**: Burg 13, 8000 Brugge
- **Phone**: +32 50 44 87 11
- **What to See**: A small but significant church that houses a relic believed to be the blood of Christ. It's a peaceful and historically important site in Brugge.

4. Groeningemuseum

- **Address**: Dijver 12, 8000 Brugge
- **Phone**: +32 50 44 87 11
- **What to See**: This museum features an impressive collection of **Flemish Primitive** paintings, including works by **Jan van Eyck** and **Hans Memling**.

5. Canal Tours

- **Where to Book**: Canal boat tours depart from **Rozenhoedkaai** and **Dijver**.

- **Cost**: €10-€12 for a 1-hour boat ride.
- **What to See**: A relaxing and scenic way to see Brugge's historic canals and picturesque buildings.

Directory of Key Services

1. Tourist Information Centers

- **Address**: Stationsplein 4, 8000 Brugge (near Brugge Station)
- **Phone**: +32 50 44 46 46
- **What to Expect**: The official **Tourist Information Center** provides maps, brochures, and information about things to do in Brugge. The staff can also help with bookings for tours and activities.

2. Hospitals and Medical Services

- **AZ Sint-Jan Hospital**
- **Address**: Bruggesteenweg 4, 8000 Brugge
- **Phone**: +32 50 45 45 11
- **What to Expect**: This hospital is the main medical facility in Brugge and provides emergency and routine medical care.

3. Police Station

- **Address**: Dijver 17, 8000 Brugge
- **Phone**: +32 50 44 88 10
- **What to Expect**: If you need assistance with any emergency, the local police are available. They also assist with lost property.

4. Embassy Services (for international visitors)

- **US Embassy in Brussels**

- **Address**: Boulevard du Régent 27, 1000 Brussels
- **Phone**: +32 2 811 40 00
- **Website**: https://be.usembassy.gov
- **UK Embassy in Brussels**
- **Address**: Regentlaan 1, 1000 Brussels
- **Phone**: +32 2 287 60 11
- **Website**: https://www.gov.uk/world/belgium

Travel Resources and Further Reading

For those looking to dive deeper into Brugge's culture, history, and attractions, there are several excellent resources available.

1. Official Brugge Tourism Website

- **Website**: www.visitbruges.be
- **What It Offers**: This is the best place to start for official information on events, attractions, tours, and accommodations in Brugge.

2. Books about Brugge

- **"Bruges and Ghent: The Rough Guide to Belgium and Luxembourg"** A great travel guide that covers Brugge and other Belgian cities, providing practical advice on where to go and what to see.
- **"Bruges: A Cultural History" by P. H. A. J. (Pieter) Jansen** For those interested in the rich history of Brugge, this book dives deep into the city's cultural and historical past.

3. Travel Blogs

- **"The Culture Trip – Brugge"**: A blog offering detailed suggestions for things to do and see in Brugge, including hidden gems.
- **"Brugge Uncovered"**: A local blog that provides insights into off-the-beaten-path activities in Brugge.

4. Mobile Apps

- **Visit Brugge App**: Offers maps, recommendations, and up-to-date details about events and attractions.
- **Google Maps**: Helpful for navigating Brugge, finding attractions, and even checking transport schedules.

Printed in Great Britain
by Amazon